LUMEN

The Catholic Gift
to Civilisation

Revised Edition

Fr. Marcus Holden MA (Oxon), STL

Fr. Andrew Pinsent MA (Oxon), DPhil, STB, PhL, PhD

Catholic Truth Society

Scriptural citations in this booklet are taken from the Revised Standard Version (RSV) Catholic Edition. The abbreviation "ccc." followed by a number indicates a paragraph from the *Catechism of the Catholic Church*.

The range of subjects covered in this booklet makes a list of further reading impractical. Among recent publications, however, the authors recommend Thomas E. Woods, *How The Catholic Church Built Western Civilization*, Regnery Publishing (2005) and James Hannam, *God's Philosophers: How the Medieval World Laid the Foundations of Modern Science*, Icon Books Ltd (2009). Although neither of these works was used to compile *Lumen*, they are motivated by similar concerns and contain much more detailed accounts of some of the same kinds of topics, together with references for further reading.

The publisher acknowledges permission to reproduce the following: - Pg 6: Albert Einstein with Robert Millikan and Georges Lemaître © Bettmann/Corbis. Pg 10: Abraham Ortelius, Time & Life Pictures/Getty Images/Buyenlarge/Getty Images. Pg 14: De Dondis Astrarium, the world's first astronomical clock, 1364. SSPL via Getty Images © SSPL/Science Museum. Pg 18: Baptistery of Grado: Interior © Vanni Archive/Corbis. Pg 22: Stained glass windows from the St. Nicolas church in Amsterdam © ictor/ iStockphoto. Pg 26: Last Judgment by Fra Angelico © The Gallery Collection/Corbis. Pg 30: Wall Painting of Saint Thomas Aquinas© Alinari Archives/Corbis. Pg 34: Italian City of Assisi © Gianni Giansanti/Sygma/Corbis. Pg 42: A woman teaching geometry, 1350. Artist: Unknown © The British Library / Heritage-Images. Pg 46: Mosaic of Christ with Angels from the Basilica of Santa Prassede in Rome © Araldo de Luca/Corbis. Pg 50: Sagrada família 4 © Rainer Walter Schmied/iStockphoto. Pg 54: Hot cross buns in a basket, next to wooden chicken and painted eggs © Dorling Kindersley/Getty Images. Pg 58: Mother Teresa of Calcutta at her Mission in Calcutta, India © Tim Graham/Corbis. Pg 62: The Rest on the Flight into Egypt After Raphael © Christie's Images/Corbis. Pg 66: Wall paintins in Voronet Monastery, Gura Humorului, Romania © Marco Cristofori/Corbis. Pg 70: A Baptism Scene, from 'Decrets de Gratien' (vellum) by French School, (13th century) Bibliotheque Municipale, Laon, France/ Giraudon/ The Bridgeman Art Library. Pg 74: Visitation From the Life of Christ Lancet Window at Chartres Cathedral © Dean Conger/Corbis. Pg 78: Human Fetus © Frans Lanting/Corbis. Pg 82: Pope John Paul II in Poland © Henri Bureau/Sygma/Corbis. Pg 86: Saint Cyril and Saint Methodius © The Art Archive/Corbis. Pg 90: William Shakespeare © Heritage Images/Corbis. Pg 94: An Initial from Pius II Book of Psalms © David Lees/Corbis. Pg 98: The Pope asks forgiveness for the sins of the church © PIZZOLI ORI/CORBIS SYGMA. Pg 102: Detail of Paradise from Last Judgment by Fra Angelico © The Art Archive/Corbis.

(For those images where identifying copyright has been unsuccessful, the publisher would be grateful for information to trace copyright ownership).

Contents

Light for the Mind

Light from the Sacraments

3

Light for the Moral Life

Light from Prayer

A Prayer of St Thomas Aquinas
who always prayed before study

Bestow upon me, O God, an understanding that knows you, wisdom in finding you, a way of life that is pleasing to you, perseverance that faithfully waits for you, and confidence that I shall embrace you at the last. Amen.

Introduction

In a recent debate, broadcast worldwide by the BBC, over 87% of the audience *rejected* the motion that the Catholic Church is a force for good in the world. Whatever the many plausible reasons for this outcome, it suggests that there is little awareness of the contributions of the faith to civilisation.

To set the record straight, this booklet summarises the extraordinary enlightenment that Catholicism has brought to the world. Much of our university system, art, music, legal tradition, charity and even a great deal of our science have come from Catholic civilisation and Catholic minds. While whole libraries would be required to explore these topics in detail, surprisingly little of what is contained in this booklet is widely known, to judge from public debates and the media. Besides encouraging Catholics and supporting those involved in catechesis, this booklet may therefore be of great interest to teachers and the general enquirer of some faith or none.

The division of sections follows loosely the fourfold structure of the *Catechism*, with the twenty-five sections corresponding approximately to those of the *Evangelium* course, *Credo* pocket catechism and *Apologia*, also published by the Catholic Truth Society. The title of the booklet, '*Lumen*' ('light') signifies an attempt to reclaim for the faith the notion of enlightenment. The ultimate inspiration, however, comes from the words of Jesus Christ, "*Let your light shine before others, so that they may see your good works and give glory to your Father in heaven*" (Mt 5:16).

Fr Georges Lemaître, 'Father of the Big Bang' with Robert Millikan and Albert Einstein, California Institute of Technology, Pasadena, January 1933

In 1927, Fr Georges Lemaître published a paper in the *Annals of the Scientific Society of Brussels* presenting the idea of an expanding universe and a derivation of Hubble's Law, which predicted that the recessional velocity of distant galaxies would increase in proportion to their distance. When invited to a meeting of the British Association in London in 1931, Lemaître proposed that the universe had expanded from an initial point, which he called the 'Primeval Atom'. In 1949, Prof. Fred Hoyle described Lemaître's theory as a 'Big Bang'. So although this fact is rarely mentioned by mass media today, a Catholic priest founded the most important theory of modern cosmology.

Light and the Cosmos

"In the beginning God created the heavens and the earth. The earth was without form and void, and darkness was upon the face of the deep ... And God said, 'Let there be light'; and there was light." Gen 1:1-3.

The Catholic record

Catholics have made a remarkable contribution to the study of light and the cosmos. The *Opus Maius* (1267) of a Franciscan friar at Oxford, **Roger Bacon** (d. 1292), written at the request of Pope Clement IV, initiated the tradition of optics in the Latin world. This early work is also notable for its emphasis on empirical, experimental methods and the role of mathematics in understanding the physical world.

Shortly after Bacon's work, the first **spectacles** were invented in Italy sometime around 1300 (the earliest pictorial evidence for the use of spectacles is a painting in 1352 of a cardinal, Hugh de Provence, reading in a scriptorium). These **convex lenses** were used to alleviate the problems of both hyperopia (farsightedness) and presbyopia (inability to focus on close objects). Cardinal **Nicholas of Cusa** (d. 1464) is believed to have been the first to discover the benefits of **concave lenses** for the treatment of myopia (shortsightedness) in 1451. Besides the alleviation of considerable suffering from poor eyesight, the theory and production of such instruments laid the foundation for the development of the combinations of lenses and mirrors used in telescopes and microscopes.

Optics and practically every other field of science benefited from the work of **Leonardo da Vinci** (d. 1519), the supreme exemplar of the intellectual and artistic creativity of Catholic Italy during the Renaissance. In the 16C, a Catholic cleric, **Nicolaus Copernicus** (d. 1543), proposed **heliocentrism**, according to which the earth and planets orbit the sun. A century later, the Church refused to allow heliocentrism to be treated as more than a hypothesis, since conclusive proof was lacking and the theory seemed opposed to the literalistic sense of Scripture. When **Galileo Galilei** (d. 1642) broke the terms of an agreement to present a balanced account of the competing theories (and also appeared to ridicule Pope Urban VIII, who had actually supported him), he was forced to recant and works advocating heliocentrism were censored. Nevertheless, Galileo himself was not treated too severely. He subsequently lived first as a guest of the Archbishop of Siena, and then confined to his villa where he carried on writing, eventually dying of old age. His daughter became a nun. As further discoveries strengthened the case for heliocentrism, culminating in Bessel's measurement of stellar parallax (1838), the Church dropped all residual censorship. This case cannot, therefore, be treated as evidence for a general state of warfare between science and religion, as has so often been claimed.

Catholic basilicas with meridian lines were used as **solar observatories** in the 17C and 18C to confirm the accuracy of the new Gregorian calendar. **Fr Giuseppe Piazzi** (d. 1826) discovered the first minor planet, **Ceres**, in 1801. **Fr Angelo Secchi** (d. 1878) helped to found **astrophysics** by inventing instruments for analysing the spectra of the sun and other stars, and by developing the first system of **stellar classification**. At this time, Fr Secchi was director of the **Vatican Observatory**, which still carries out research today.

The modern understanding of light and electromagnetism owes much to Catholics, including **Alessandro Volta** (d. 1827), who developed the electric battery and the first long-distance electrical communication, and the devout **André-Marie Ampère** (d. 1836), the father of electrodynamics. **Fr Ruđer Bošković SJ** (d. 1787) laid the foundations of **field theory**, modelling atomic behaviour in terms of forces.

Most dramatically, the modern theory of cosmology, the **Big Bang theory**, was invented by a priest, **Fr Georges Lemaître** (d. 1966). Fr Lemaître was honoured by the Pope, who appointed him to the Pontifical Academy of Sciences (1936). By contrast, while atheists often claim to be the allies of science, the Soviet Union, founded on an atheist ideology, condemned the Big Bang as a reactionary theory helping clericalism, opposition that continued until the 1960s.

Catholicism, light and the cosmos: the deeper connections

Catholicism teaches that all things, visible and invisible, have been created by God. So to explore the universe is to explore God's handiwork, a spiritual motivation that is denied to those who view science purely as a means to material benefits.

Since the faith also teaches that God is a Trinity of reason and love, the Catholic mind expects to discover order in the universe, giving hope to the enterprise of cosmic exploration.

Finally, the clerical origin and warm reception of the Big Bang theory by the Church also shows how Catholic teaching about creation has freed us to theorise about the causation and change of the cosmos as a whole, rather than simply accepting the cosmos as an eternal, unchanging given.

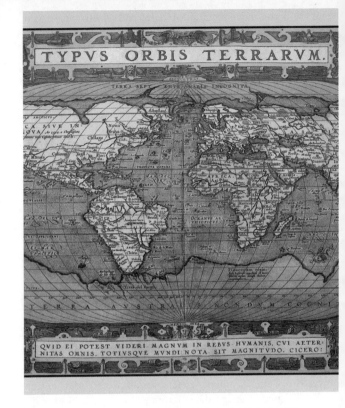

*The Typus Orbis Terrarum, by Abraham Ortelius, published in 1570,
from a book of maps that is regarded as the first modern world atlas*

The work of Ortelius was a landmark of the Age of Exploration, a period
during which Catholics from Europe undertook a series of great voyages of
discovery, establishing direct contacts with unexplored regions of Africa, the
Americas, Asia, Oceania and producing the first scientific maps of the planet.

Earth and Nature

"And he said to them, 'Go into all the world and preach the gospel to the whole creation ...'" Mark 16:15. *"This gospel of the kingdom will be preached throughout the whole world ..."* Matt 24:14.

The Catholic record

Catholic civilisation has made a remarkable contribution to the scientific investigation and mapping of the earth. In the high Middle Ages, **Marco Polo** (d. 1324) explored Asia on a journey that took 24 years and covered 15,000 miles. The great **Age of Exploration** began with the Portuguese Prince **Henry the Navigator** (d. 1460) who organised a series of voyages down the west coast of Africa. Subsequent explorers included **Bartolomeu Dias**, who rounded the southern tip of Africa (1488), **Columbus**, who sailed the Atlantic and found the Americas (1492) and **Magellan's** expedition of 1519–1522, which included the first crossing of the Pacific and the first circumnavigation of the globe. To put these achievements in context, neither the Chinese nor Ottoman empires, with similar technology, undertook comparable explorations.

Along with exploration, Catholics were largely responsible for **mapping the world**. As well as many schematic *mappae mundi* during the Middle Ages, such as that of Hereford (13C) and the Fra Mauro map (c. 1450), the Catholic world produced **the first modern scientific map**: Diogo Ribeiro's *Padrón Real* (1527) based on empirical observations of **latitude** made on the voyages of discovery. Cartography was later advanced by the work of the Catholic astronomer Giovanni Cassini (d. 1712), the first to make measurements of **longitude** using eclipses of the satellites of Jupiter as a clock.

Catholics also played leading roles in the foundation of geology. Georg Pawer (d. 1555) earned the title '**father of mineralogy**' for his great work *On the Nature of Metals*. Fr Nicolas Steno (d. 1686) was the founder of **stratigraphy**, the interpretation of rock strata which is one of the principal foundations of **geology**. In particular, he is credited with the law of superposition, the principle of original horizontality, and the principle of lateral continuity, which provide the basis for reconstructing the natural history of rocks.

With regard to living things, monastic orders played a key role in the Middle Ages in developing and applying **agriculture**, turning much of Europe's inaccessible and overgrown wilderness into cultivated land. Although evolution is today associated most with Darwin, it was **Jean-Baptiste Lamarck** (d. 1829), a French Catholic, who developed the first theory of **evolution**, including the notion of the transmutation of species and a genealogical tree. The Augustinian monk **Fr Gregor Mendel** (d. 1884) founded **genetics** based on studying the inherited characteristics of c. 29,000 pea plants (1856 – 1863). Mendel also pioneered the application of mathematics and statistics to biology, and his laws of inheritance revolutionised the cultivation of plants and the breeding of animals. Notably, while atheists often claim to be the true friends of science, advocates of Mendelian genetics were persecuted in the Soviet Union, the first state officially based on an atheist ideology. Some of these scientists, such as Nikolai Vavilov (d. 1943), died in concentration camps.

Catholicism, earth and nature: the deeper connections

A possible reason why Catholic civilisation has been fruitful in world exploration is precisely because the faith is 'catholic', that is, **universal**, and because of Christ's commission to the Church to "*go into all the world*" (Mk 16:15) and to teach and Baptise all nations (cf. Mt 28:19). Many religions are closely linked to particular peoples or regions, and even many Christian communities outside the Catholic Church are closely tied to particular countries, cultures or regions. By contrast, Catholic Christianity has no such limits. The faith spread from Jewish to Gentile converts in the first century, then from the Greek to the Latin world and then beyond the limits of the former Roman Empire to the Celts, Saxons, Indians and so on. The devotional practice of pilgrimage has also helped to reinforce this universality, which does not mean that the faith seeks to abrogate or replace local cultures. On the contrary, the faith adopts and transfigures whatever is good. Examples of this transfiguration can be seen in Chinese icons of Mary and Jesus today or the image *Our Lady of Guadalupe* (1531) in which Mary's clothing draws from Aztec symbolism.

The fruitfulness of the faith with regard to agriculture and the natural world may be related to Catholic understanding that holiness is **cultivated**, principally by prayer, the sacraments and an ordered life fruitful in good works. By analogy, this idea of cultivation may also be extended to the world in general, underpinning the notion of a gradual 'unfolding' (*evolvere*) of the natural order from seminal principles without contradicting God's sovereignty or the **doctrine of Creation**. Tempered by certain cautions, the Magisterium has not, therefore, regarded evolution as incompatible with the faith.

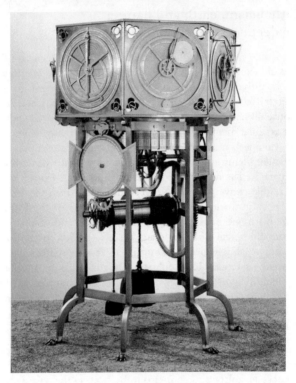

A reconstruction of the Astrarium, an elaborate medieval clock displaying the main elements of the solar system together with religious and civil calendars

The *Astrarium*, completed in 1364 by Giovanni de Dondi after sixteen years work, is recognised as a marvel of precision and beauty. This elaborate clock, with its planetary dials, circular and elliptical gears and link mechanisms, shows the extraordinary advances in computation and precision engineering being made in Catholic Europe in the 14C. These advances provided the basis for many subsequent developments in science and technology.

History and Time

"The Church is in history, but at the same time she transcends it. It is only 'with the eyes of faith' that one can see her in her visible reality and at the same time in her spiritual reality as bearer of divine life." ccc. 770.

The Catholic record

The word 'history' is linked to the idea of a narrative or story. Unlike many religious works, the central books of Christian revelation, the four Gospels, are **narratives** and not, for example, lists of proverbs or commands. Indeed, the Gospel of Luke describes itself as a narrative taken from reports of eyewitnesses (Lk 1:1-4). So the genre of **historical writing** was present from the very beginning of the Christian faith.

The early Church considered her own **historical continuity** to be a vital sign of authenticity, as shown in records of the **apostolic succession** of bishops. In c. 180 AD, for example, St Irenaeus listed the bishops of Rome in unbroken succession from the time of Peter and Paul (*Against Heresies*, III.3). Eusebius of Ceasarea (d. 339), the 'Father of Church History', used a narrative genre for his *Ecclesiastical History*. He also established the popularity of the **chronicle** (events arranged by a time line) and the **universal chronicle** (a chronicle of the entire world). The use of **annals** (annual records) became widespread from the 7C. Records from parishes and monasteries are invaluable for their long-term continuity, being used today for studying family trees and even climate.

The many great Catholic historians over the centuries include **St Bede the Venerable** (d. 738), the 'Father of English History', the **Ven. Cardinal Baronius** (d. 1607) and **John Lingard** (d. 1851), who argued that one of his chief duties as an historian was, "*to weigh with care the value of the authorities on which I rely, and to watch with jealousy the secret workings of my own personal feelings and prepossessions.*" Recent Catholic historians include **Christopher Dawson** (d. 1970) and **Eamon Duffy**, who have transformed our understanding of the cultural role of religion and the history of the Reformation. The continuity of the faith has also enabled extraordinary acts of collective scholarship, such as the work of the **Bollandists**, lasting for three centuries (1643-1940), to compile histories of the saints.

Along with history, Catholic civilisation has also been fruitful in the philosophy and measurement of time. St Augustine (d. 430) was perhaps the first to grasp that **time is relative**, arguing that it does not make sense to ask what God was doing 'before' Creation (*Confessions*, XI.13). Boethius (d. 524) gave a definition of **eternity** as "*the complete possession all at once of endless life*" (*Consolation*, V.VI). From the early Middle Ages, Church bells marked the passage of time and the **first clocks with mechanical escapements** (producing a characteristic 'tick-tock') were used in cathedrals, monasteries and town halls by c. 1200. Subsequent, highly complex clocks, such as Giovanni de Dondi's *Astrarium* (1364), stimulated the development of mechanics and precision engineering. The Catholics Luigi Lilio (d. 1576) and Fr Christopher Clavius SJ (d. 1612) were the main architects of the **Gregorian Calendar** (1582), named after Pope Gregory XIII and now the principal calendar of the world. Finally, the faith has also provided a central, fixed reference point for time, dividing history into BC (before Christ) and AD (in the year of the Lord).

Catholicism, history and time: the deeper connections

There are several probable reasons why the faith has been fruitful with regard to history and time. First, while sins are forgiven instantly, for example in Baptism or Confession, growth in holiness is generally more gradual, as shown in Jesus' parables about sowing and reaping. Since holiness is **cultivated** rather than manufactured, **time** and a disciplined, **regular life** are of great help. A regular life, however, requires the marking of hours and liturgical seasons, for which clocks and records are important. Furthermore, fixing the date for the liturgy of Easter (the first Sunday after the full moon after the northern hemisphere's vernal equinox), was a strong incentive to develop an accurate, universal calendar.

Second, the faith holds that holiness consists in friendship with God. Friendship, however, is usually cultivated over time and the literary genre most suitable for **knowing a person** (as opposed to a set of instructions) is the narrative genre, as in the Gospels. Hence Christians have had a strong sense of the importance of narrative history from apostolic times.

Third, the **Incarnation** has shaped our understanding of time on the cosmic scale. Many ancient societies regarded time as cyclical, repeating eternally like the cycles of the stars. From this fatalistic perspective, *"there is nothing new under the sun"* (Eccl. 1:10). By contrast, as Fr Stanley Jaki (d. 2009) has argued, the Incarnation breaks this dreary circle, and time is now being 'folded in' towards a conclusion (cf. 1 Cor 7:29). So for Christianity time is **linear**, an understanding that underpins the notion of 'progress'. In other words, past and future are not the same, as in a circle, but distinct, as for seed growing towards harvest.

Interior of the Baptistry of Grado (late 5C) in north-eastern Italy

The construction of these elaborate buildings highlights the great importance attached to Baptism, by which a person becomes born again as an adopted child of God, enjoying a new and supernatural life of grace.

The Human Person

"First, the common good presupposes respect for the person as such. In the name of the common good, public authorities are bound to respect the fundamental and inalienable rights of the human person." ccc 1907.

The Catholic record

The word '**person**' and derivative words like '**personal**' and '**personality**', used in everyday conversation, are themselves fruits of the faith. It is true that there was a word *persona* in classical Latin, but this word originally meant 'mask'. The word *hupostatis* in Greek, which became the word for 'person', originally covered a wide range of meanings, including 'standing under', 'foundation' and even 'jelly'. The modern meanings associated with the term 'person' emerged through the process of articulating the Catholic understanding of the Trinity and Jesus Christ. In the terminology of St Gregory Nazianzus, which Pope St Damasus I affirmed (382), the Trinity is 'one substance, *three persons.*' The Council of Chalcedon (451) confirmed Catholic teaching about Jesus Christ being '*one person,* two natures: human and divine'.

Besides the divine Persons, Catholic Christianity has also applied the term 'person' to **all human beings**. St Thomas Aquinas (d. 1274) wrote, *"An individual of human nature is a 'hupostasis' and a person"* (SCG, IV.43). Attributing personhood to all human beings implies that they share in an adoptive sense in the holiness of God, reinforcing the sanctity of life.

This link between Catholic theology and the treatment of persons has been fruitful in many other ways. For example, each of the Divine Persons of the Trinity is not *a* person (one of many) but a *particular person*, with unique relationships in the Godhead. Applied more generally, this uniqueness of persons is one reason why great variety, of persons and institutions, has been one of the hallmarks of Catholic civilisation. Furthermore, the diversity of the saints (men, women, children, kings, beggars, slaves and so on), witnesses to a Catholic sense that God regards each person as unique.

Yet another fruitful connection between Catholic theology and the human person has been in **art** (see p. 47). Western art, which largely developed under Catholic influence, has given a unique emphasis to the **face** and the **hands**, those parts of the body most expressive of a personality. Famous examples include the portraits of St Thomas More by Holbein (d. 1543) and the *Mona Lisa* of Leonardo da Vinci (d. 1519). This emphasis is in contrast to pagan classical art, which emphasised the exterior form of the body, and to Islamic culture, which has often encouraged faces to be veiled and forbidden the artistic representation of the human face.

Due to its Catholic foundation, the concept of a person and corporate personality are woven deeply into the Western legal tradition. By contrast, anti-Christian movements often restrict or downplay the term 'person'. Communist movements, for example, tend to refer to 'the people' rather than persons. In the West, the term 'person' is gradually being limited to those who are visible, healthy and articulate, one consequence of which has been widespread abortion and embryo destruction. A professor at Princeton, Peter Singer, has even argued that infanticide is not morally equivalent to killing a person.

Catholicism and the human person: the deeper connections

The root cause of the prominent role of persons in Christianity is that the consistency of Revelation requires the need for what is denoted by the word **'person'**. When Jesus Christ says, "*I and the Father are one*," the 'one' refers to the 'substance' of God, expressed in the **Creed** by the words "*of one being with the Father.*" Jesus also refers to 'I' and the 'Father' as distinct, however, revealing that a *person* is distinct and superior to the classical notion of substance. Without the category of 'person', Catholic theology would be impossible, because philosophy lacks the tools to express all the necessary distinctions and relationships of God and the Incarnation.

A person, however, is not just a superior kind of being to which special moral laws apply. A person is **relational**. When St Augustine (d. 430) writes, "*Late have I loved you, O Beauty ever ancient, ever new, late have I loved you! You were within me, but I was outside, and it was there that I searched for you. ... You touched me, and I burned for your peace.*" (*Confessions* X.27), he addresses God in the kind of language that was unknown to pagan philosophers. Aristotle, for example, only refers to God in the third person. St Augustine, by contrast, addresses God as 'you' (the second person) and writes of himself in the first person in a way that has earned him the title, 'Father of Autobiography.' By means of Baptism, by which we become adopted children of God and brothers and sisters of Jesus Christ, Christianity has brought about an 'I'-'You' or *second-personal* relationship with God that also changes how we perceive other beings in the world. In the light of this relationship, other human beings are not individual, isolated egos, cogs or consumers, but persons to whom we are related as our brothers and sisters.

A depiction of the Holy Trinity in stained glass, from a window in the St Nicolas church in Amsterdam (1886), possibly designed by Jan Coenraad Bleijs (d. 1952)

Due to the Incarnation, the 'Word made flesh', it is possible to represent the second person of the Holy Trinity in art without idolatry, and to represent the other divine persons in relationship to him. Such images are symbols of the good news, namely that it has become possible to know and love the Holy Trinity personally and not merely to know about God as a distant creator.

The Holy Trinity

"Go therefore and make disciples of all nations, baptizing them in the name of the Father and of the Son and of the Holy Spirit, teaching them to observe all that I have commanded you." Matt 28:19-20.

The Catholic record

The Catholic faith teaches that the one God is three persons, Father, Son and Holy Spirit. Properly speaking, all things are fruits of the Trinity, but the **revelation of the Trinity** is a fruit of the faith, insofar as belief in the Trinity is unique to Christianity. Furthermore, there are certain cultural fruits that are closely associated with the way in which the Trinity permeates the Christian understanding of God.

One important cultural fruit of the Trinity is in terms of what is attributed to God. Outside of Christianity, the attribute most naturally associated with God is that of **power**, and God is often perceived as inscrutable, remote and perhaps without love. The Trinity, by contrast, shows that God is a God of **reason** (Jesus is described as the 'Word') and that the most important attribute of God is **Love**, an attribute associated with the union of divine persons and especially with the Holy Spirit. Hence St John says, *"God is Love"* (1 Jn 4:8), and he draws a strong connection between loving, in the Christian sense, and knowing God (1 Jn 4:7). Across many different ways of life, it is this ideal of love which is the foundation of Christian morality, laws and vocation.

In addition, there is a special fruitfulness associated with the particular designations of each divine person. To call God **'Father'**, not simply in an honorific way, but from the point of view of someone adopted as a child of God in Baptism, is radically different from thinking of God simply as a patron or source of benefits. In the case of **God the Son**, the narrative accounts of the New Testament give us intimate knowledge of a person with whom **divine friendship** is possible, *"No longer do I call you servants, for the servant does not know what his master is doing; but I have called you friends"* (Jn 15:15). By contrast, the pagan philosopher Aristotle had claimed that we cannot be friends with God because of the gulf that exists between God and human beings (*Nicomachean Ethics*, VIII, 7, 1158b33 – 1159a3). Similarly in Islam, the idea that we can enjoy friendship with God (as opposed to being rewarded for righteous conduct) is rare, even if it is present at all. Finally, the images associated with **God the Holy Spirit**, especially fire and the dove, convey qualities that inform the ideal Christian life: fire signifies fervour, the dove signifies simplicity (in contrast to guile) and both symbols, in different ways, signify **love**. The teaching that the Holy Spirit is a person also prevents the Spirit being thought of as some impersonal force or source of power.

The indirect fruits of these attributions and images inform many of the topics covered in other sections of this booklet. They inform, for example, Christian art, literature, morality, society, the family, virtues and the law. Many symbols, such as the Shamrock, are Trinitarian, and many educational and social institutions are dedicated to the Trinity. The preamble to the Irish Constitution of 1937 begins, *"In the Name of the Most Holy Trinity, from Whom is all authority and to Whom, as our final end, all actions both of men and States must be referred."*

Catholicism and the Trinity: the deeper connections

The Trinity is not rooted in anything but is the origin of all things. Nevertheless, there are reasons why the Catholic faith was able to articulate and defend the doctrine of the Trinity.

First, the Church was able to preserve, transmit and guarantee the **Scriptures** in which the roots of belief in the Trinity are found. As St Augustine wrote, "*I would not believe in the Gospel, had not the authority of the Catholic Church already moved me*" (Contra Epistolam Manichaei 5, 6 (ccc. 119)). Scripture reveals that Jesus is God (cf. Jn 20:28; Mk 2:1-12), but also describes him as the only begotten Son (Jn 1:14; Heb 1:5). The Holy Spirit is linked to the Father and the Son in the formula of Baptism (Matt 28:19-20) and a blessing used in the Mass, "*The grace of the Lord Jesus Christ and the love of God and the fellowship of the Holy Spirit be with you all*" (2 Cor 13:14). The Holy Spirit is also described in personal terms, such as being a counselor (Jn 14:26; Jn 16:13), not an impersonal force.

Second, great saints of the early Church gave doctrinal shape to belief in the Trinity, their work being tested and recognised by the Church. **St Athanasius** (d. 373), for example, defended the full divinity of Jesus Christ, while **St Gregory of Nyssa** (d. late 4C) defended the divinity of the Holy Spirit.

Third, the Catholic faith affirms that God is not contrary to **reason**. So although philosophy cannot prove the Trinity, reason can highlight incomplete understanding. For example, a principle called the 'Identity of Indiscernibles' is consistent with the need to distinguish the Son and the Spirit in some way, a need that is met by the Catholic teaching that the Spirit uniquely proceeds from the Father and the Son.

The resurrection from the dead, centrepiece of The Last Judgment by Fra Angelico, painted c. 1430 and now in the museum of San Marco in Florence

This image illustrates the fruitfulness of the Catholic understanding of salvation and eternity. The sense in which our response to God's gift of salvation shapes our eternal destiny has had a profound impact on art, music, literature, the moral life and many other aspects of Catholic civilisation.

Salvation and Eternity

"We would not have you ignorant, brethren, concerning those who are asleep, that you may not grieve as others do who have no hope ... through Jesus, God will bring with him those who have fallen asleep." 1 Thes 4:13-14.

The Catholic record

The *Epistle to Diognetus* (c. 2C), describes the Christian life as follows, *"Though destiny has placed them here in the flesh, they do not live after the flesh; their days are passed on the earth, though their citizenship is above in the heavens."* This epistle shows how early Christians behaved like pilgrims in this world, rejoicing in being freed from sin, anticipating the resurrection and looking forward in hope to living with God forever in heaven.

This view of salvation and eternity shapes the way people view the 'story' of their lives. For example, early Christians worked with a kind of **extravagant freedom**, knowing that they were spreading the message of salvation and not relying on this brief life for their only hope of happiness. These principles helped to motivate the work of great **missionaries**, such as **St Paul**, the 'Apostle to the Gentiles', **St Patrick** (d. 493), the 'Apostle of Ireland', and **St Francis Xavier** (d. 1552), who made pioneering visits to Japan, India, Borneo and the Moluccas. Yet to focus on heaven invariably proves to be a blessing for this world as well. Along with spreading the faith, such work has been bountiful in terms of languages and cultures, even founding cities and entire nations.

Belief in salvation and eternity has also been fruitful in less obvious ways than great missionary journeys. Since Christ laid down his life for others, **sacrificial love** has been a consistent Christian ideal. This principle has inspired a celibate priesthood, a view of marriage as a covenant and many other ways of life in which a person is consecrated to God. The numerous associations supporting a consecrated life include Augustinians, Benedictines, Carmelites, Dominicans, Franciscans, Jesuits and Salesians. These associations have themselves had an incalculable effect on civilisation, preserving libraries and encouraging learning, music, art and practical charity. Many religious orders today, such as the Missionaries of Charity, carry out spiritual and practical work in some of the poorest and most dangerous places worldwide, including the decayed inner cities of wealthy countries.

The themes of salvation and eternity have also shaped much of the world's great literature and art, including the **Divine Comedy** of Dante (d. 1321) and the **Last Judgement** of Michelangelo (d. 1564). In the 15C, the ***Ars moriendi*** ('The Art of Dying') addressed the meaning of a good death in the light of salvation and eternity. This work established a new literary genre, providing assistance and consolation to those preparing to die and portraying death as the culminating action of a life rather than a disaster. Similar motivations underpin the **modern hospice movement**, which values human life to the point of natural death, in contrast to those who judge that certain lives are not worth living. The hope of eternal life and Resurrection can also be seen in **prayers for the dead**, such as 'Rest in Peace (RIP)' on gravestones. A miracle that is consistent with these beliefs is that the bodies of certain saints (called **'incorruptibles'**), such as Saint Bernadette (d. 1879), have not decayed in the normal way.

Catholicism, salvation and eternity: the deeper connections

Salvation and eternity are themes that permeate Scripture, tradition and the lives of the saints. In particular, the **death and Resurrection of Christ** proclaims that the price has been paid for our salvation, confirms personal immortality and offers the promise of a glorified risen humanity.

The Catholic understanding of salvation, however, also emphasises that co-operation with God's love shapes our eternal life (see p.105). Although salvation is an undeserved gift, **we are free to accept or reject that gift**. More subtly, the choices we make can influence the **kind of saints** we become. St Paul illustrates this point when he tells us that this life becomes the **seed** of our eternal state (cf. 1 Cor 15:38). In addition Jesus himself says, *"Whoever gives to one of these little ones even a cup of cold water because he is a disciple, truly, I say to you, he shall not lose his reward."* (Matt 10:42). In other words, even the smallest deed in union with divine love will shape our eternal destiny. C. S. Lewis expressed this connection as follows, *"In this life we write the title page of what we are to be in eternity."*

This understanding of salvation and eternity has had a profound influence on how Catholics seeking to become saints have lived and shaped civilisation. They have not sought to earn salvation from God, which is impossible, but they have been **extravagant in their sacrifices** to **give God glory** and increase their own **joy in union with him**. St Thérèse of Lisieux (d. 1897) wrote, *"My God, I choose everything – I will not be a saint by halves. I am not afraid of suffering for Thee. One thing only do I fear, and that is, to follow my own will. Accept then the offering I make of it, for I choose all that Thou willest!"*

An image of St Thomas Aquinas (d. 1274), an Italian priest of the Dominican Order who is widely regarded as the Church's greatest philosopher and theologian

The work of St Thomas Aquinas exemplifies the Catholic conviction that human reason, enlightened by God, can and should be applied to matters of faith. His courtesy in presenting and responding to the best arguments of his opponents also sets the standard for how academic debate should be conducted without violence or polemic. Much of modern philosophy was developed either in opposition to Aquinas or in agreement with his ideas, particularly in the areas of ethics, natural law and political theory.

Philosophy and Theology

"Not acting reasonably is contrary to God's nature ... Whoever would lead someone to faith needs the ability to speak well and to reason properly, without violence or threats." Benedict XVI, Regensburg Address.

The Catholic record

Philosophy is the 'love of wisdom' and wisdom deals with first causes and principles. Questions like, *"What is knowledge?"* or *"What is being?"* or *"Is there a God?"* belong to philosophy. Philosophy developed in Greece over the period 6C to 3C BC, the most influential philosophers being Plato (d. 347 BC), our source for Socrates, and Aristotle (d. 322 BC).

Catholicism regards philosophy as intrinsically good. The faith has drawn greatly from Greek philosophy and has itself stimulated new philosophical insights. The early Christian St Justin Martyr (d. 165) saw hints of God's revelation in the insights of Socrates. The word *homoousious*, translated as 'consubstantial' or 'of one being' in the Creed, is from Greek philosophy. **St Augustine** (d. 430) drew from Plato and made many novel contributions, stimulating, for example, the study of the will. **St Thomas Aquinas** (d. 1274), absorbed and transfigured the philosophy of Aristotle. The many other Catholic philosophers include **St Anselm** (d. 1109), **Bl Duns Scotus** (d. 1308), **Suárez** (d. 1617) and **Blaise Pascal** (d. 1662). Recent figures include **St Edith Stein** (d. 1942), **Elizabeth Anscombe** (d. 2001) and **Alasdair MacIntyre**.

Philosophers not only ask questions but also propose answers that can have far reaching effects upon how we view the world, society and ourselves. Catholic thinkers have been active in defending the following principles: that the **human person** is irreducible to matter and has an immortal soul; that human persons have **free will**, and do not simply act like machines; that the **virtues** are important for human perfection and happiness, unified by divine love (*caritas*); that God has created beings that can be the causes of their own actions, i.e. **secondary causation**; that certain things, especially living things, have **natures** or **final causes**; that there is **objective good and evil** and **natural law**, rooted in the nature of things; that **matter is good**, not intrinsically evil; the **principle of non-contradiction**, one meaning of which is that opposite statements cannot both be true.

In addition, Catholics largely founded **theology**, the discipline of applying reason to what has been revealed supernaturally. Unlike religious revelations that are lists of divine commands from some distant deity, or a mix of chaotic and incredible stories, Catholic thinkers have worked on the basis that God is a **God of reason** and that the truths that He reveals fit together in a coherent, extraordinary way. The discipline of uncovering this order is called 'theology', which St Anselm described as *'faith seeking understanding.'* On one hand, theology helps protect religion from fundamentalism. On the other hand, by making revelation credible to reason, theology also helps to oppose cold rationalism without faith. Beyond uncovering ordered truths about God's revelation, however, theology also seeks to describe what it means to know and love God, in the sense of an 'I'-'You' (second-personal) relationship, the fruit of which is **friendship with God**.

Catholicism, philosophy and theology: the deeper connections

The link between philosophy and faith can be traced to many sources in Scripture. For example, philosophers often refer to God in terms of Absolute Being, the same language that was also used in the Old Testament when God revealed His name to Moses, "*I am who am*" (Ex 3:14). Furthermore, philosophy is the love of wisdom and the Catholic Old Testament includes an entire book devoted to wisdom, personified as a woman beloved of God. In the New Testament, Jesus repeats the 'I am' phrase of Exodus (John 8:58), once again bringing to mind an association between the God of Revelation and the Absolute Being of philosophy. St John also refers to Jesus as the *Logos*, meaning 'word', 'ordering principle' or 'reason' (John 1:1), highlighting an essential harmony between God and reason.

The link between the faith and theology may be rooted in the kind of relationship that the Catholic faith believes that God has established with us. By means of Baptism, we become adopted **children of God**, partakers of the Divine nature (2 Pet 1:4) and members of the Church. A child is not an instrument or slave, following orders from a remote deity without hope of making sense of these orders. On the contrary, since God has willed to become Our Father as well as our creator, it is reasonable to trust that he wants us to understand – and that he has made it possible for us to understand – what he has revealed. As Jesus says, "*No longer do I call you servants, for the servant does not know what his master is doing; but I have called you friends, for all that I have heard from my Father I have made known to you*" (John 15:15). According to this passage, knowing God and loving God are intimately linked, implying the possibility and value of theology in helping us to seek the face of God.

*The centre of Siena, a city in Tuscany that formed the nucleus of an
independent city-state until the middle of the sixteenth century*

The city-states of Italy between the tenth and fifteenth centuries were the
centres of the Renaissance, a period of great development in the arts, sciences
and commerce. The many distinct societies in Italy during this period witness
to the great cultural diversity of Catholic civilisation.

Christian Society

"There is a certain resemblance between the unity of the divine persons and the fraternity that men are to establish among themselves in truth and love. Love of neighbour is inseparable from love for God." ccc. 1878.

The Catholic record

The origins and development of many societies have been interwoven with the Church. **Armenia** became the first Christian state in 301. The concept of **France** originates with the reign of Clovis (c. 511), the first Catholic King of the Franks. The consciousness of **England** as a nation owes much to the work of members of the Church such as Bede (see p. 16). Charlemagne's empire and the **Holy Roman Empire** were closely connected with the Church. Similarly, the histories of many societies today have strong Catholic influences, one sign of which can be seen in place names like Maryland, San Francisco, São Paulo and San Salvador.

These examples reveal that Catholic societies tend be richly **diverse**. Indeed, this diversity is seen not only at the level of the state but in a vast array of associations distinct from the state, such as Church leadership, families, parishes, dioceses, religious orders, universities, corporations and guilds. Paradigm examples of this rich diversity were the **city-states of Italy** between the 10C and 15C, including Venice, Milan, Florence, Pisa and Siena. Despite many feuds, these states produced a **mercantile, professional class** and were the centre of the **Renaissance**, a period of great development in the arts, sciences and commerce. By the 13C, northern and central Italy was also the most literate society in the world.

Besides promoting culturally rich societies, Catholicism has also articulated and defended three key principles of political philosophy: **human dignity**, **solidarity** and **subsidiarity**. Human dignity and solidarity are closely related principles based on the intrinsic value of the human person (see page 19) and an ethic of union among persons. An important defense of these principles was the encyclical *Rerum Novarum* (1891) on the conditions of labour, which opposed unfettered capitalism and defended a living wage. The principle of subsidiarity was first developed by Fr Oswald von Nell-Breuning (d. 1991) and articulated further in an encyclical of Pope Pius XI, "*One should not withdraw from individuals and commit to the community what they can accomplish by their own enterprise and industry*" (*Quadragesimo Anno*, 79). Subsidiarity opposes state socialism, unnecessary centralisation and any tendency to reduce persons in society to the role of cogs in a machine.

Consistent with the principles of subsidiarity and human dignity, Catholic thinkers have also promoted **distributism**, a third-way economic philosophy. According to distributism, the ownership of the means of production should be spread as widely as possible among the general populace, rather than being centralised under the control of the state (state socialism) or a few large businesses or wealthy private individuals (plutocratic capitalism). A summary of distributism is found in Chesterton's statement, "*Too much capitalism does not mean too many capitalists, but too few capitalists*" (*The Uses of Diversity, 1921*). The Catholic convert E. F. Schumacher (d. 1977), who wrote *Small is Beautiful*, was greatly influenced by this philosophy.

Catholicism and Christian society: the deeper connections

The way in which Catholicism has shaped diverse societies may be due, first, to the nature of the Church herself. The Church is not like a machine, with an all-powerful leader pulling levers and individuals being moved like cogs. On the contrary, the Church is better described by living analogies, like those of a **body**, **flock** or **garden** (*Dei Verbum*, 5, 6). The Magisterium governs principally to nurture the garden and protect it from whatever might inhibit its fruitfulness. What comes forth from the garden, however, is often unexpected: Pope Innocent III (d. 1216), for example, supported St Francis (d. 1226) but had not expected him or his vocation. As an organic, not mechanistic, society, it is not surprising that the Church has promoted solidarity and subsidiarity.

A second principle is that of **distinct powers of governance**, articulated by Christ's injunction, "*render unto Caesar the things which are Caesar's, and unto God the things that are God's*" (Matt 22:21). The Church regards the state as an essential natural good for human flourishing. Yet the Church also maintains that she is distinct from the state and has a divine commission to govern in matters pertaining to salvation. This distinction has helped to inspire many other separations of powers in societies.

Finally, the most important principle of Catholic social impact is *caritas*, or '**divine love**', according to which all human beings are potentially or actually children of God and one's brothers and sisters. Whatever the failings of Catholics to live up to this teaching, it is this supernatural relationship, not contingent mutual advantage, that ultimately underpins the Catholic ideals of social cohesion and solidarity.

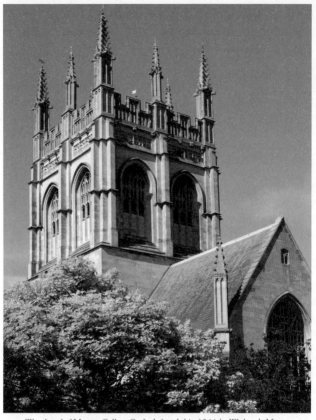

The chapel of Merton College, Oxford, founded in 1264 by Walter de Merton, sometime Chancellor of England and later Bishop of Rochester

The university system is one of the great achievements of Catholic civilisation. There were over fifty universities in Europe by the middle of the fifteenth century.

Education

> "*Let us learn whatever can be learnt from man; and let him who teaches another communicate what he has himself received without arrogance and without jealousy.*" St Augustine, *On Christian Doctrine*, Preface 5.

The Catholic record

From its earliest days the Church has held education in high regard. In about 107 AD, St Ignatius of Antioch, the first person in history to use the phrase 'Catholic Church', wrote, "*It is good to teach, if he who speaks also acts,*" (*Ephesians* 15) and "*A righteous father educates [his children] well*" (*Philadelphians* 4). Even amid intermittent persecution, early Christians founded schools such as the Catechetical School of Alexandria (c. 190).

With the breakdown in civil society following the collapse of the Roman Empire, the **monastic system** played a crucial role in preserving texts, libraries and education. An early example was that of Cassiodorus (mid 6C), who established a *scriptorium* to collect, copy, and preserve texts. Of even greater importance was the form of monastic life established by Saint Benedict (d. c. 547), a pattern that spread throughout Europe and beyond. The monastery at Montecassino, for example, preserved several classical texts, such as the later *Annals* and *Histories* of Tacitus, texts that might otherwise have been lost forever. From the seventh century, Catholic civilisation also produced a system of **cathedral schools**. Indeed, what may be the oldest still extant school in the world, The King's

School in Canterbury, may have originated with an abbey founded by St Augustine of Canterbury himself in 597.

Perhaps the greatest single contribution to education to emerge from Catholic civilisation was the development of the **university system**, the word *universitas* being used to describe specialized associations of students and teachers with the status, in law, of corporate personality. The *Authentica Habita* (1155), written by Emperor Frederick I Barbarossa and confirmed by Pope Alexander III, extended a clerical status to scholars to grant them legal protections and freedom. Early Catholic universities include Bologna (1088); Paris (c. 1150); Oxford (1167); Salerno (1173); Vicenza (1204); Cambridge (1209); Salamanca (1218-1219); Padua (1222); Naples (1224) and Vercelli (1228). By the middle of the fifteenth century, (more than seventy years *before* the Reformation), there were already over **fifty universities in Europe**. Many of these universities, such as Oxford, still show signs of their Catholic foundation – such as quadrangles modelled on monastic cloisters, gothic architecture and numerous chapels.

Catholic scholars in the twelfth and thirteenth centuries translated many newly discovered (or re-discovered) works in Greek and Arabic into Latin. Around 1440, Catholic civilisation also produced the **movable type printing press** system of Johannes Gutenberg. This invention made the mass production of books and tracts possible. The first book printed in this way was an edition of the Bible translated by St Jerome, the Vulgate. Greek texts, both classical and Christian, were also soon printed for the first time.

After the Reformation, the Church lost much of her educational infrastructure in many countries. In recent centuries, however, it has been possible to begin to build new institutions in these countries. At the time of writing, about 10% of children in England are educated in Catholic schools, and these schools tend to be oversubscribed.

Across the world, **Church schools** today educate more than fifty million students and provide much of the educational infrastructure in many developing countries. Benazir Bhutto (d. 2007), the first woman elected to lead a Muslim state, was one of many to benefit from education at a Catholic school.

Catholicism and education: the deeper connections

The command of Christ himself to teach all nations shows that teaching is central to the work of the Church. Furthermore, the Gospel ('Good News') is, of its nature, **'new'**, that is it contains elements that have to be transmitted through teaching. The ancient Greek philosophers knew that there is a God, but would not have guessed that God would be born in a stable. Such *supernatural* truths have to be taught, handed on from one generation to the next. Hence, **teaching** is essential along with all the **apparatus of teaching**, such as schools, colleges, libraries and manuscripts. For this reason, the Catholic Faith is intimately associated with education.

With regard to natural knowledge, the complaint is sometimes made that Christians regarded many pagan works with suspicion and that some works were lost, usually through lack of interest or carelessness. What was preserved most carefully, however, was refined literature and philosophy, while the many gaudy and irrational aspects of paganism in the ancient world were largely lost. Paradoxically, therefore, our exalted view of the classical world itself reflects the priorities of Christian communities towards **wisdom and learning**.

An illuminated manuscript (1308-1315) of Euclid's Elements, now in the British Library, showing a medieval woman teaching geometry to a group of monks

Images of women in the Middle Ages, which include the first self-portraits by women artists, women reading, playing instruments and teaching, show that Catholic civilisation during this period had a respect for a woman's potential and dignity that differs greatly from popular views of the Middle Ages.

The Status of Women

"My soul magnifies the Lord, and my spirit rejoices in God my Saviour, for he has regarded the low estate of his handmaiden. For behold, henceforth all generations will call me blessed." Luke 1:46-47.

The Catholic record

The idea that the Catholic faith has enhanced the status of women might seem strange, given that popular prejudice is to believe the opposite. Yet the Church has given unique honour to a woman, **Mary**, above all the saints and honoured her with the title, **Mother of God**, (Council of Ephesus, 431). Women were the **first witnesses of the Resurrection** (Mk 16:1-11; Mt 28:1-10; Lk 24:1-11; Jn 20:1-18), supported **early missionary work** (Rom 16:1, 6; Phil 4:2), and **passed on the faith** as **mothers** and **grandmothers** (2 Tim 1:5). In contrast to pagan society, which considered widowhood to be a curse, Scripture mentions **widows** being given help and an active role in the early Church (Acts 6:1-2; 9, 39).

Many women, such as **Ss Blandina**, **Felicity**, **Perpetua**, **Agnes**, **Cecilia** and **Lucy**, were honoured greatly for their love and courage in dying for the faith in the first three centuries. **St Fabiola** (d. 399) built a hospice for the sick, arguably the first hospital in Rome. **St Clotilde** (d. 545) helped to bring her husband, Clovis, to Baptism, the first milestone of the history of France, and **St Bertha** (d. c. 612) helped to introduce Christianity to Anglo-Saxon England.

From at least the foundation of the community of Saint-Jean in Arles, in 513, the faith gave the world a woman unknown to classical antiquity: **the nun**. Great nuns of the Middle Ages include: **St Hilda** (d. 680), after whom St Hilda's College, Oxford is named, who was founding abbess of a monastery at Whitby and adviser of kings; **Herrad of Landsberg** (d. 1195), author of an encyclopaedia, and **Bl Hildegard von Bingen** (d. 1179), abbess and polymath, who left over 100 letters, 72 songs, seventy poems, and 9 books. While women in monastic life were often well educated, the benefits of female education spread more widely. The *Manual for My Son*, written by a noblewoman called **Dhuoda** (c. 843) is arguably the oldest known **treatise on education**, and there are records from the Middle Ages (such as at Notre-Dames de Saints in 1148) showing that convents customarily educated girls and boys. In **caring for the sick**, the work of **Bl Mother Teresa** (d. 1997) follows a tradition going back to the early Church. Florence Nightingale (d. 1910), for example, learnt about the care of wounded soldiers during a year spent with the **Sisters of St Vincent de Paul** in Egypt.

In political life, **queen consorts**, from at least **Elfrida** (d. c. 1000) were crowned and anointed as well as their husbands, and certain women become politically powerful in their own right. These included **Empress Matilda** (d. 1167), the first woman to rule England, and **Eleanor of Aquitaine** (d. 1204). Whatever the judgment of her reign, the **first queen regnant of England**, **Mary I** (d. 1558), was devoutly Catholic.

In spiritual life, the Church recognises three women saints as Doctors of the Church: **Catherine of Siena** (d. 1380), **Teresa of Ávila** (d. 1582) and **Thérèse of Lisieux** (d. 1897).

Perhaps most surprising, Catholic civilisation produced many of the **first women scientists**. The *Passionibus Mulierum Curandorum* (*The Diseases of Women*), attributed to **Trotula of Salerno** (11C) became one of the key medical works of the Middle Ages. **Dorotea Bucca** (d. 1436) occupied a chair in medicine at the University of Bologna for over forty years. **Anna Mazzolini** was a Professor of Anatomy at the University of Bologna in 1760. Other notable pioneers include **Elena Lucrezia Piscopia** (d. 1684), the first woman to receive a Doctor of Philosophy degree (1678) and **Maria Agnesi** (d. 1799), the first woman to become Professor of Mathematics at any university, and who was appointed to that position by a Pope, Benedict XIV, in 1750.

Catholicism and the status of women: the deeper connections

Catholic civilisation has scarcely always been enlightened towards women and misogynistic statements can be found even by great teachers of the faith. Nevertheless, Catholicism is arguably unique among monotheistic religions in combining strong feminine as well as strong masculine aspects. The root of this emphasis may be the recognition of Mary as the '**second Eve**' in the early Church (St Irenaeus, *Against Heresies*, V.19). Furthermore, although the Church is 'patriarchal', in the sense that ordained ministers are men and men are the heads of families, this kind of leadership is radically different from the patriarchy of paganism. In pagan Rome, the man exercised the power of life and death over his family (a modern instance of which is so-called 'honour killing'). In Christianity, by contrast, the ideal of fatherly leadership is that of **St Joseph**: a leadership of sacrifice and service unto death to enable the flourishing of his wife and family.

Mosaic of Christ with Angels
from the Basilica of Santa Prassede in Rome

Art

"Concerning the word of life – the life was made manifest, and we saw it, and testify to it, and proclaim to you the eternal life which was with the Father and was made manifest to us." 1 Jn 1:1-2.

The Catholic record

Early evidence that art has been a fruit of the faith dates from early inscriptions on catacombs. The frescoes of the baptistry of the house-church at **Dura-Europos**, which include Christ as the 'Good Shepherd' and Christ and Peter walking on the water, date back to c. 235. **Christian mosaics, stone carvings** and **painting** flourished after the legalisation of Christianity (313). An almost complete Roman mosaic dating from the 4C, which almost certainly portrays Jesus Christ, was discovered in 1963 at Hinton St Mary in Dorset and is now in the British Museum. This mosaic and many other early Christian artefacts display the **'Chi-Rho' symbol** (the first two Greek letters for Christ). There are also Christian mosaics from the 4C in the church of **Santa Pudenziana** in Rome.

The painting of **icons**, from the Greek for 'image', typically of Christ and the saints, dates from at least the 5C. According to St Bede in his *Ecclesiastical History* (731), when St Augustine landed in England in 597 he arrived with a large processional crucifix and icons, bringing art as well as faith. The earliest surviving Christian **panel icons**, dating from the 6C, are at the monastery of St Catherine in Sinai. Panel painting later developed into highly sophisticated works such as *The Ghent Altarpiece* by Jan Van Eyck and his brothers (1432).

While the ancient Romans produced coloured glass, **pictorial stained glass** is a uniquely Christian innovation. From the 10C to the 15C, stained glass was probably the main pictorial art form in northern France, Germany and England.

Giotto (d. 1337) is credited with initiating a new realism in painting, developing techniques of **drawing accurately from life**, using **perspective** devices and **expressing emotions** through his depictions of the **human face**. One of the fruits of these developments, by Giotto and his contemporaries, are the frescoes of the **Basilica of St Francis** in Assisi. The promotion of nativity scenes and 'Stations of the Cross' by the Franciscans also helped to inspire new three dimensional art and drama. **Brunelleschi** (d. 1446) is credited with inventing one-point linear perspective in painting, with **Alberti** (d. 1472) explaining the mathematical theory.

The work of **Bl Fra Angelico** (d. 1455), today the patron saint of art, expressed theological insights, especially those of St Thomas Aquinas, using the new methods of the High Renaissance. Subsequent centuries in Catholic Italy produced the unrivalled work of **Leonardo da Vinci** (d. 1519), **Raphael** (d. 1520), **Caravaggio** (d. 1610), **Michelangelo** (d. 1564) and **Bernini** (d. 1680). Many of the works of these artists, such as Michaelangelo's **Sistine Chapel ceiling** are considered among the greatest works of art of all time.

In modern times, **Cristo Redentor** (1934), an Art Deco statue of Christ, has become the principal symbol of Brazil. Other contemporary works inspired by the faith include the **Redemptoris Mater chapel** (1999) in the Vatican.

Catholicism and art:
the deeper connections

In the Old Testament and ancient Judaism, images were associated with the danger of idolatry, since there was a risk that people would worship what they had made, as in the story of the golden calf (Exod. 32). For this reason, graven images were prohibited in the Ten Commandments. A similar fear of idolatry is generally believed to be behind much destruction of representational art (iconoclasm) in the history of Islam. Indeed, fear of idolatry has even driven some Christians, including certain emperors in 8C and 9C Byzantium and certain Protestants in 16C and 17C Europe (such as the Puritans in England) to destroy much religious art.

The reason why Catholicism has taken a different stance is rooted ultimately in the **Incarnation**. St John of Damascus (8C) wrote, "*I boldly draw an image of the invisible God, not as invisible, but as having become visible for our sakes by partaking of flesh and blood*" (On the Divine Images, First Apology). In other words, the Incarnation has made representational art potentially holy, insofar as such art does not represent idols but Christ and what belongs to him. This position was officially confirmed by the **Second Council of Nicaea** (787), which strongly endorsed the religious importance of representational art, "*As the sacred and life-giving cross is everywhere set up as a symbol, so also should the images of Jesus Christ, the Virgin Mary, the holy angels, as well as those of the saints and other pious and holy men be embodied in the manufacture of sacred vessels, tapestries, vestments, etc., and exhibited on the walls of churches, in the homes, and in all conspicuous places, by the roadside and everywhere, to be revered by all who might see them.*" This edict gave official and strong support to the subsequent development of art in the Catholic world.

The Sagrada Família in Barcelona, designed by Antoni Gaudí (d. 1926) and consecrated 7 November 2010 by Pope Benedict XVI.

Architecture

"Say to the householder, 'The Teacher says, "Where is my guest room, where I am to eat the passover with my disciples?"' And he will show you a large upper room furnished and ready." Mark 14:14-15.

The Catholic record

Archaeological discoveries have shown that early Christians had the desire to construct sacred buildings, at least when this was possible while living under intermittent persecution. Legalisation of the faith (313) was quickly followed by a great flowering of church architecture. The **Emperor Constantine** (d. 337) sent his mother **St Helena** (d. 330) to preserve and turn the sacred places in the Holy Land into shrines and he gave land on the Lateran hill to build the first great Christian cathedral, the **Basilica of St John Lateran** (324). Other great basilicas of the 4C/5C include **St Peter's** on Vatican Hill, **St Mary Major**, and **St Paul Outside the Walls**.

A new Christian city, **Constantinople** (330), the nucleus of what became the **Byzantine Empire**, provided the opportunity to develop Byzantine architecture. This style emphasised mosaics, domes and interior beauty, expressing the Christian theme of the inner illumination of the soul. The church of **Hagia Sophia** (6C) is still remarkable for its massive dome and use of light. From 8C to 13C, Christian architecture in the West blended elements of Roman and Byzantine buildings to create the **Romanesque** style, characterised by its massive quality, round arches, large towers and decorative arcading. The many extant Romanesque buildings include **Speyer Cathedral** (11C) and **Tournai Cathedral** (12C).

From the 13C, **Gothic architecture**, with its pointed arch, the ribbed vault and flying buttress, removed the need for massive, load-bearing walls. These innovations transformed much of the interior surface of buildings like **Sainte-Chapelle**, **Cologne Cathedral** and **York Minster** into curtains of light filtered through **stained glass windows**, another Christian development dating from at least the 7C. The gothic style was revived in 19C England, partly in response to the ideas of the Oxford Movement, and can be seen in the design of the **Palace of Westminster**. One of the architects of this project, **A. W. Pugin** (d. 1852), testified that gothic architecture helped bring about his own conversion to Catholicism. Pugin went on to design seven cathedrals and forty churches, and the fruits of neo-gothic revival can be seen in many buildings today, including **São Paulo Cathedral** (1954) and the main building of the **University of Glasgow** (a university founded by a bull of Pope Nicholas V in 1451).

Renaissance architecture, with a strong emphasis on the mathematical proportion and classical order, developed from the 15C in Catholic Italy. The greatest works of **Brunelleschi** (d. 1446), **Bramante** (d. 1515), **Michelangelo** (d. 1564) and many others were designed for the expression and use of the Catholic faith and were made possible by Catholic funding.

The **Church of the Gesù** (1584), the mother church of the Jesuit order, became the prototype of **Baroque architecture**, which gave a special emphasis to dramatic imagery. The use of large-scale ceiling frescoes, strong contrasts and opulent ornaments was in deliberate contrast to early Protestant movements, which frequently whitewashed walls and avoided images. Great Baroque architects include **Borromini** (d. 1667), **Pietro da Cortona** (d. 1669) and **Bernini** (d. 1680).

On 7 November 2010, Pope Benedict XVI consecrated the Basilica of the **Sagrada Familia**, the culminating work of the devout architect **Gaudi** (d. 1926). The Sagrada Familia, which blends Gothic and Art Nouveau designs, shows that the faith continues to be an inspiration for highly original architecture.

Catholicism and architecture: the deeper connections

A root of the Catholic emphasis on sacred architecture can be seen in the extraordinary care and devotion given to the **Temple** of the Old Testament. The Temple was the place of authentic sacrifice, but also the place of the presence of God, "*I was glad when they said to me, 'Let us go to the house of the Lord*'" (Ps. 122:1). According to Catholic teaching, the Church is the new Israel and every particular church is a place where the **Sacrifice of the Mass** is offered and where **God is present**, in the sacramental form of the hosts in the tabernacle. So just as the Temple of the Old Testament was magnificent, Catholics have held that it is fitting to put great effort and creativity into buildings for the Mass and other sacraments.

Furthermore, bishops exercise their ministry as **successors of the apostles**, a role prefigured by the 'judges' of Ancient Israel, "*In the new world ... you will also sit on twelve thrones, judging the twelve tribes of Israel*" (Matt 19:28). As a cathedral is a 'chair' (*cathedra*) of a bishop, it is fitting that these buildings should express the authority and beauty of Christ's kingdom.

*Hot cross buns and Easter eggs, modern foods that are closely
linked to events of the liturgical calendar*

Food and Drink

"Jesus spoke to them in parables, saying, 'The kingdom of heaven may be compared to a king who gave a marriage feast for his son, and sent his servants to call those who were invited to the marriage feast.'" Matt 22:1-3.

The Catholic record

Many kinds of food and drink have their roots in Catholic civilisation and certain foods are closely linked to the liturgical calendar. **Hot cross buns** are associated with Lent, with the cross being a symbol of Christ's cross. The ingredients of **mince pies** were often associated with the events of Christmas (such as cinnamon, cloves and nutmeg symbolising the three gifts of the Magi) and these pies were regarded as sufficiently Catholic to be banned by English Puritans. **Christmas pudding** originated from the medieval dish of *frumenty*, a spicy, wheat-based dessert used for saints' feast days. The **cappuccino** is named after the Capuchin friars.

Viniculture, the branch of horticulture devoted to wine, is interwoven with Catholicism, being inherited from the ancient Romans and developed, especially by monasteries, for the sake of the Mass. In Burgundy, the Cistercian monks invented the place-based classifications of '**terroir**' and '**cru**', based on long term observations of areas that would consistently produce wines of similar aroma, body, colour and vigour. Some of the most famous wines have explicit Catholic connections. **Châteauneuf-du-Pape** is named after the

Papacy, which was in Avignon in the 14C and sponsored the local cultivation of wine. **Dom Pérignon** (d. 1715), after whom the famous champagne is named, was a Benedictine monk at Hautvillers who improved the quality of grapes used for wines and reduced imperfections in the fermentation process. **Viniculture in the Americas** began with the cultivation of 'mission grapes' from Spain, introduced to the western coasts of North and South America by missionaries for use making sacramental, table, and fortified wines.

The earliest written evidence for the **distillation of alcohol** can first be traced to the 12C medical **School of Salerno**, with **fractional distillation** (now an essential tool of chemistry and the petrochemical industry) first described by **Tadeo Alderotti** of Florence (d. 1295). By the beginning of the 14C, monks had spread knowledge of distillation methods for making **whiskey** to Scotland and Ireland. The *Liber de arte distillandi de compositis* by **Hieronymus Brunschwig** (c. 1512) describes the use of distilled alcohol as medicine, and is one of the earliest books on chemistry and pharmacology.

Some of the finest **liquors** in the world come from the monastic tradition. **Chartreuse**, made from a complex (and secret) blend of herbs, flowers and other ingredients in a wine base, was first developed for medicinal reasons by the monks of Grande Chartreuse, the Carthusian monastery founded by St Bruno (d. 1101). Another famous liquor, **Benedictine**, was named in 1863 by Alexandre Le Grand, who sought to recreate the famous medicinal beverage of **Fécamp Abbey** after the abbey had been disbanded following the revolution.

Many religious houses had **brewhouses** in the Middle Ages and, at a time when water was often dirty, drinking **beer** often helped to reduce disease. A Carolingian abbot recorded the first known addition of **hops** for stability and flavouring (c. 822). **St Bernard's Cistercian order** was well known for its brewing and beers from Trappist abbeys, such as **Chimay**, are still popular today. Many other famous beers, such as **Leffe**, first brewed by the Norbertines of the abbey Notre Dame de Leffe (1152), are now brewed commercially. The link between Catholicism and brewing is also underlined by **St Arnold of Metz** (d. 640), a patron of beer, who is honoured each July with a parade in Brussels on the 'Day of Beer'.

Catholicism, food and drink: the deeper connections

Due to the Incarnation and sacraments, the Catholic faith recognises that what is **utterly holy** has been given to us in a **material, concrete form**. Since the means of salvation are given in this material way, Catholicism is radically opposed to that view called 'Manichean', according to which the material world is intrinsically evil. While there are, of course, spiritual dangers from gluttony and drunkenness, the faith does not regard food and drink as being tainted or evil in themselves.

Furthermore, the **Eucharist** is the source and summit of the Christian life and is in the form of a sacred meal. As a result, a certain sanctity carries over to everyday meals, with the development of specialised food and drink encouraged by the fasts and feasts of the liturgical calendar. Traditional meals in Catholic societies, blessed by prayers and good company, therefore have sacramental and liturgical connotations that stand against the culture of 'fast food' and disordered consumption. Scripture also describes several key events when Jesus ate and drank, thereby blessing these activities, and often describes heaven as a wedding feast (Rev 19:9).

Blessed Mother Teresa (d. 1997), who founded the Missionaries of Charity in Calcutta and spent nearly fifty years caring for the sick and dying

Care for the Sick and Dying

"Whatever you did for one of the least of these brothers and sisters of mine, you did for me" (Mt 25:40). *"Let them call the priests of the Church to pray over them (the sick) and anoint them with oil."* Jam 5:13.

The Catholic record

Care for **the poor, the sick and dying** has been considered one of the marks of saintly Christians since the early Church. St Ambrose (d. 397), when teaching the duties of the clergy, relates the story of St Lawrence, the deacon martyred c. 258. When the Roman authorities demanded that he surrender the treasures of the Church, he pointed to the poor he had gathered and said, *"These are the treasures of the Church."* Subsequent devotion to St Lawrence highlights the way in which the faithful have recognised his priorities as exemplary.

After 313 the Church was free to work more openly and charitable care increased rapidly. Canon 70 of the First Council of Nicaea (325) mandated that **hospitals** should be established in every city. About 370 **St Basil of Caesarea** (d. 379) established a religious foundation that included a hospital, an isolation unit for those suffering from leprosy, and buildings to house the poor, the elderly, and the sick. Following this example similar hospitals were later built in the eastern part of the Roman Empire. In the West, chapter 36 of the **Rule of St Benedict** (d. 547), which established the framework for subsequent monastic life across Europe, begins, "*Before all things and above all things, care must be taken of the sick, so that they will be served as if they were Christ in person.*"

In 660 the first hospital in the city of Paris was founded by its bishop, **St Landry** (d. c. 661). In the Middle Ages, these French hospitals were called '**Hôtel-Dieu**' meaning 'hostel of God', the name indicating their religious inspiration. The first Spanish hospital was founded by the **Bishop Masona** in 580 at Mérida. In Jerusalem, the work of caring for poor, sick or injured pilgrims led to the founding of the **Knights Hospitaller** (1113), the successor of which, the **Sovereign Military Order of Malta**, carries out extensive humanitarian work to the present day. In London, **St Thomas' hospital**, named after St Thomas Becket, was established before 1215. **St Bart's** was founded in 1123 by Rahere, formerly a courtier of Henry I, following a vow made while on pilgrimage. The **Royal College of Physicians** was founded in 1518 by the Catholic scholar and priest Thomas Linacre (d. 1524).

Catholics also constructed the first hospitals in the Americas, including the **Hospital San Nicolás de Bari** (1503) and what is now the **Hospital de Jesús Nazareno** (1524) in Mexico City. Canada's first hospital, **Hôtel-Dieu of Québec**, was completed in 1639 and run by French Augustinian nuns.

In more recent times, the work of **Bl Teresa of Calcutta** (**Mother Teresa**) (d. 1997) inspired an order operating 610 missions in 123 countries by the time of her death, caring for the poor, the sick and the dying. The experience of working at St Joseph's Catholic Hospice in Hackney for several years led an Anglican, Dame Cicely Saunders (d. 2005) to found the **modern hospice movement**. In the year of his conversion to the Catholic faith (1948), **Sir Leonard Cheshire** (d. 1992), founded what is now called **Leonard Cheshire Disability**, which provides support to disabled people throughout the world. His Catholic wife **Sue Ryder** (d. 2000) has also given her name to several important charitable institutions.

Catholic institutions also collectively provide the largest single contribution to caring for AIDS sufferers. Where Catholic sexual ethics has been promoted, as in the Philippines, the rate of AIDS infection tends to be comparatively low.

In support of care of the sick, mention should also be made of medical research. In Catholic Italy, the **School of Salerno**, from the early 10C, became the **first medical school** and **Mondino de Luzzi** (d. 1326) in Bologna introduced dissection of cadavers, founding modern anatomical research. **Hieronymus Fabricius** (d. 1619) at Padua was the father of **embryology**, and also taught William Harvey, who is normally credited with discovering blood circulation. The Papal physician **Marcello Malpighi** (d. 1694), discovered the capillaries linking arteries and veins.

Catholicism and care for the sick and dying: the deeper connections

Jesus' care and healing of the sick has set the primary example for Christians to follow. Furthermore, he has warned that at the Last Judgment he will consider care, or neglect, of the sick or needy to have been done to him (cf. Mt 25). What inspires genuine care by saintly persons, however, is the principle that every human being is actually or potentially one's brother or sister in grace, children of the same heavenly Father. This attitude is very different from treating a person simply as a complex biological machine, or as a unit of economic production. For someone who truly loves God, care for the sick and dying is not only natural, but even a privilege.

The Rest on the Flight into Egypt after Raphael (16C)

Images of the holy family typically portray the child Jesus as the focus of attention, followed by his mother Mary and finally his foster-father Joseph. This order of dignity is the precise reversal of that of the pagan families of Imperial Rome, showing how the faith transformed family relations. While Joseph is the head of the family, his leadership is one of service rather than autocratic power, and the love that unifies the family is marked by sacrifice.

The Family, Marriage and Children

"For this reason a man shall leave his father and mother and be joined to his wife, and the two shall become one flesh. This mystery is a profound one, and I am saying that it refers to Christ and the church." Eph 5:31, 32.

The Catholic record

The Church has always upheld the great dignity of marriage (CCC 1601), holding that the relationship of Christ with his Church is reflected in **sacramental marriage** between a man and a woman (Eph 5:31-32). Much of the history of Catholicism, marriage and the family traces the defence of this sacrament. The main opposing view, found in the ancient world and in many societies today, has treated marriage as little more than a contract to exchange goods, with women and children sometimes reduced to the status of possessions themselves.

Christianity began to influence the marriage and family laws of ancient Rome after the Emperor Constantine gave the faith official recognition. In 331, the emperor imposed serious penalties on unilateral divorce, except in extreme cases of misconduct. In 374, Roman law mandated that **every child born must be reared**, a striking contrast to ancient laws that a child had no civic status unless recognised by the father. With practical help provided by the Christian development of **orphanages**, especially by religious orders, infanticide, either direct or as a result of abandonment, became virtually extinct in Christian countries, at least until modern times.

In 673, the **Council of Hertford**, presided over by **St Theodore** (d. 690), decreed that marriage is only allowed between **one man and one woman**, separation is only granted in the case of adultery, and remarriage is not allowed, a pattern of legislation that was followed across medieval Europe. In defence of the sacrament of marriage, especially the rights of women under threat of divorce, the Church was even willing to confront monarchs. **Pope Nicholas the Great** (d. 867) overturned an annulment given to Lothair II of Lotharingia simply because his wife was barren and he desired to marry his concubine. **Pope Clement VII** (d. 1534) similarly refused to allow Henry VIII of England an annulment from Catherine of Aragon, a decision that was extremely costly in political terms. Many leaders of the Reformation, by contrast, did not recognise marriage as a sacrament but as a civic matter, and in 1540 Martin Luther even condoned the bigamy of Philip of Hesse. The Church continues to defend the uniqueness and indissolubility of sacramental marriage today, against a rising tide of divorce and a new wave of anti-Christian legislation that seeks to compel society to give equal status to homosexual unions.

Catholic sacramental marriage has also had profound cultural impact beyond legislation. Unlike a contractual view of marriage, in which a human being is valued for providing certain benefits, a covenant is a loving union of persons. This sacramental understanding of marriage, associated with the sacrifice and joy of the saints, has inspired much literature on the theme of courtship and the medieval Catholic ideals of **chivalry**, from which the term **'romance'** originates. By contrast today, as society treats marriage simply as a contract to exchange goods, and as sexual immorality of various kinds has increased, the romance of marriage has also faded.

Catholicism and the family, marriage and children: the deeper connections

The sacramental understanding of marriage, characterised by love, sacrifice and indissolubility, can be seen in the way that **St Paul** likens the joining of man and wife to the relationship of Christ and his Church (Eph. 5:31-32). In addition, **Jesus** spoke of the **indissolubility** of marriage and worked his first miracle, at the behest of his mother, at a wedding feast (Mk 10:2-9; Jn 2:1-11). This miracle, when he turned water into wine, has also been seen as a sign of the elevation of marriage into a sacrament.

Some sense of the importance of this connection of marriage with Christ and his Church can be seen from its revolutionary understanding of the way in which a person relates to God. In paganism, divine beings are treated principally as a possible source of benefits by means of some contractual exchange. This understanding is reflected in marriage being treated as a contract that is dissoluble if either party fails to provide the goods, but in which transgressions of the contract may be punished with extreme severity. With the coming of Christ, however, the unthinkable gulf between God and humanity has been bridged. Instead of God being remote and aloof from human affairs, as in classical paganism, great Christian writers, such as St Augustine (d. 430) frequently address God as 'you', and in terms of passionate love. This new relationship to God profoundly influences Christian marriage. One cannot, for example, agree to love someone with Christian love on a temporary or conditional basis, as in a contract, and so valid marriages are indissoluble. There is also little of joy, sacrifice or forgiveness inherent to the notion of a contract. By contrast, these attributes are central to the Christian covenant with God and shape the Christian understanding of marriage.

Wall painting in Voronet Monastery, Gura Humorului, Romania

Morality and Freedom

"May our Lord Jesus Christ himself, and God our Father, who loved us and gave us eternal comfort and good hope through grace, comfort your hearts and establish them in every good work and word." 2 Thes 2:16-17.

The Catholic record

Evidence that Catholic Christianity defends an intrinsic link between faith and morality can be found from the earliest days of the faith. At the end of the first century, St Clement, one of the first bishops of Rome, wrote, *"Let us clothe ourselves with concord and humility, ever exercising self-control … being justified by our works, and not our words"* (1 Clem. 30). In other words, this early bishop taught that a Christian, having received God's forgiveness and grace, should not merely confess faith, but should **avoid evil** and be **fruitful in good works**.

Similar themes can be found throughout early writings. St Athanasius (d. 373), for example, states that *"We should serve Him (the Word) with a pure heart"* (Letter 48), emphasising the need to keep apart from moral corruption. Indeed, the refusal of early Christians to join in many of the immoral activities of the surrounding society was something that marked them out and helped to invite persecution. Yet this separation was not a cold aloofness but allied with bearing abundant good fruits in practical charity. The latter emphasis can be seen, for example, in the importance Christians have traditionally given to the **corporal and spiritual works of mercy** (see p. 59).

This emphasis on fruitfulness in good works, seen today, for example, in the work of Mother Teresa's order, has at times led to the accusation by extreme Protestants that Catholicism teaches that we earn our salvation by good deeds. In fact, the Church teaches precisely the opposite. The Council of Trent (1545 – 1563) affirmed that "*No one can be just to whom the merits of Christ's passion have not been communicated*" (D 800). Nevertheless, the Church teaches that **human freedom** has a role to play. St Augustine (d. 430) wrote that, "*God created us without us: but he did not will to save us without us*" (Serm. 169, 11, 13) and St Thomas Aquinas (d. 1274) wrote that a person is not moved by God in the manner of a slave or an inanimate instrument (ST 2a2ae q.19, a.2). A human person is therefore free to reject God's gift of grace (D 814) and in fact can do so by choosing to do something evil. More subtly, the Church also teaches that good works undertaken freely in a state of grace can merit an eternal reward (D 693), according to Christ's own promise, "*Whoever gives to one of these little ones even a cup of cold water because he is a disciple, truly, I say to you, he shall not lose his reward*" (Mt 10:42).

This Catholic view of freedom is in contrast to a surprising range of **other belief systems**. Belief in free will was eclipsed by the Reformation. For example, even Melancthon's *Loci Communes* (1521) claimed that free will was effectively non-existent and Calvin's *Institutes* (1559) claimed that God's will regarding a person's salvation is fixed and inscrutable. Free will has also been denied by many Islamic thinkers such as Al-Ghazali (d. 1111), on the basis that God is the only cause of whatever happens, and by many scientific materialists, on the basis that all change is predetermined by natural laws. In the latter case, the mistake has been to apply discoveries about simple systems uncritically to more complex cases.

Catholicism, morality and freedom: the deeper connections

Evidence for the connection of faith and morality can be found in many Scriptural texts, the most famous being the **Ten Commandments**. These moral principles are not set out and observed to buy God's favour with good deeds, however, but to preserve an 'I'-'you' (second person) relationship with God, a union of divine friendship. Hence for the Christian, the main moral danger is a false union with what is hostile to God, analogous to the betrayal of a spouse or parent. For this reason, the New Testament stresses the dangers of fornication, impurity, idolatry, sorcery, drunkenness and so on (cf. Gal 5:19-21), not primarily because they damage the order of human society (although they do) but principally because they fix the affections of our hearts on what is hostile to God and are incompatible with divine friendship.

Many of the key elements of Catholic teaching about morality and freedom can be drawn from this principle. First, we cannot earn **grace**, since we cannot earn a union of friendship with God, but can only accept this **union as a gift**, normally through the sacraments. Second, we can lose grace by certain actions, insofar as we betray God's friendship by choosing what is hostile to God. Third, with grace, that is, in a union of friendship with God, we can be fruitful in good works. Indeed, it is possible to bring in a small or a great 'harvest', depending on the extent of our surrender to God's grace – as in the 'parable of the sower' (Matt 13:3-23). Finally, since the relationship with God enabled by grace is interpersonal, this relationship **respects our freedom**. We cannot earn God's friendship, but we are free to reject the gift or to accept it and co-operate with God during the time that is given to us.

Part of a manuscript of the Concordia discordantium canonum (Concord of Discordant Canons), later simply named the Decretum, by the monk Gratian (12C)

Gratian's vast work, undertaken to reconcile seemingly contradictory canons from previous centuries, is widely regarded as the first complete, systematic body of law, in which all parts are viewed as interacting to form a whole. This text is one of the foundational documents of the Western legal tradition.

Among the many precursors of Gratian's work in Catholic civilisation is the Law of St Ethelbert. Originating in Kent in the early seventh century, this is thought to be the earliest law code of any kind in any Germanic language and the earliest surviving document written in English.

Law and Jurisprudence

"You have come to Mount Zion and to the city of the living God, the heavenly Jerusalem, and to innumerable angels ... and to God the judge of all, and to the spirits of the righteous made perfect." Heb 12:22-23.

The Catholic record

The **Western legal tradition**, which emerged in the 12C, is a fruit of Catholic civilisation drawn from several sources. First, a vast digest of legal materials compiled by the **Christian Emperor Justinian** (d. 565) came to light in an Italian library in the late 11C. Second, scholastic methods developed by **Abelard** (d. 1142) and his successors applied philosophy to particular legal cases to uncover general principles. This effort developed **jurisprudence**, the philosophy of law. Third, law was taught in the first universities, starting in **Bologna** (1088), from which the **legal profession** emerged. Finally, the reforms of **Pope Gregory VII** (d. 1085), who sought greater independence for the Church, gave impetus to forming the laws of the Church and states of Europe. Of special note was the *Concord* of the monk **Gratian** (12C), which analysed c. 3800 canons to form the **first complete, systematic body of law**, in which all parts are viewed as interacting to form a whole. These developments influenced many other fields, such as theology presented like arguments in a legal case (such as the *Summa Theologiae* of St Thomas Aquinas) and even the natural sciences, which today refer to 'laws of nature'.

The principles that emerged from this revolution still shape our laws today. These principles were **humane** in the sense that diverse elements of a human action, including **intention**, and **justice** (transcending legal technicalities) were integral to the legal framework. For example, the principle of '**good faith**' (*bona fides*) in commercial law protects the rights of an honest purchaser of goods to which the seller might not have proper title. Good faith is today a principle of international law, trade and collaborative projects like 'Wikipedia'. Another key principle was **reciprocity of rights**, underpinning, for example, equity in contract formation. Yet another principle was **universality**, seen in early 12C trans-national treaties protecting merchants and developed later into **international law** by the Dominican **Francisco de Vitoria** (1546), who defended the rights of native peoples. Procedures for judging crime and punishment were also revolutionized from the 12C. For example, **trial by jury** replaced earlier forms of trial, such as trial by ordeal, and was one of many principles protected by **Magna Carta** (1215). Another key principle was '*habeas corpus*', indicating protection from unlawful detention. Yet another principle was '*ei incumbit probatio qui dicit*', established by Cardinal Johannes Monachus (d. 1313), a maxim indicating that the prosecution has the obligation **to prove the offense beyond a reasonable doubt**. Many other Latin legal maxims used today witness to their medieval Catholic origins.

While the principles of the Western legal tradition may persist in societies that are neutral to the faith, they erode quickly in societies hostile to the faith, as happened in the totalitarian regimes of the twentieth century. Even in modern Britain, *habeas corpus* and trial by jury are examples of legal principles, established by Catholic medieval civilisation, which have been eroded or quietly suspended on certain recent occasions.

Catholicism, law and jurisprudence: the deeper connections

Catholicism regards God as a **righteous judge**, and the idea of judgment is integral to much Catholic teaching, such as the judgment of each soul upon death, purgatory, confession and penance. Furthermore, the Church is a visible society that needs governing, specifically by a shepherd given power "to bind and to loose" (Mt 16:19). So it is not surprising that Catholic civilization has taken a great interest in law and jurisprudence.

Yet even divine judgment is tempered. First, Catholic theology defends the principle that God does not act contrary to reason and that God's power does not extend to contradiction. If even God has an eternal law (or 'God is himself law', according to the preface of the *Sachsenspiegel*, the most important law book of the German Middle Ages), then earthly monarchs must also be lawful and not behave in an arbitrary and despotic fashion. Indeed, a shift towards absolute monarchy only emerged in the wake of the Reformation, for example by Henry VIII declaring himself head of the church in England (1534) and the *Kongeloven* ('King's Law') of Denmark-Norway (1665), which authorised the king to abolish all centers of power apart from himself.

Second and most important, judgment is tempered by mercy from God who is also a **loving Father**. The key parable here is that of the Prodigal Son who is welcomed back by his Father (Lk 15:11-32). This principle may have influenced the way in which the Western legal tradition usually seeks a way back for all parties from undesirable circumstances. Bankruptcy laws of the 12C, for example, protected creditors while limiting debtors' liability and protecting them from ruin.

Visitation from the Life of Christ Lancet Window at Chartres Cathedral

The image of the halo in Catholic art signifies God's gift
of the supernatural life of grace.

The Supernatural Life

"He has granted to us his precious and very great promises, that through these you may escape from the corruption that is in the world because of passion, and become partakers of the divine nature." 2 Pet 3:4-5.

The Catholic record

The word 'supernatural' originates from the expression 'above (or beyond) the natural'. In the unfolding of Catholic thought, the term 'supernatural' has acquired a special meaning, a meaning which is itself one of the principal fruits of theology and which has had a significant impact on culture.

The contrast with the word 'natural' can help to shed light on the supernatural. The **natural good life** can mean a variety of things – to the ancient Greeks it meant something like a well-ordered society, with the tranquil possession of modest earthly goods for virtuous activity, especially the higher life of the mind. Such a life, made immortal and blissful, was the pagan ideal of the Elysian Fields (*Odyssey* IV), after which the Champs-Élysées in Paris is named and which inspired Dante Alighieri's account of **Limbo** (*Inferno, Canto* IV). Some resemblance to this notion of natural happiness can be found in English ideals of the 'good life', such as a family home in the country.

God, however, is missing from this ideal of happiness, except perhaps indirectly as a remote benefactor. Indeed, the pagan philosopher Aristotle argued that we cannot be friends with God since God surpasses us in all things (cf. *Nic. Eth.*, X, 8, 1159a3-9).

By contrast, Catholicism teaches the 'Good News', not only that Christ has freed us from sin, but that he offers us a **second birth** (Baptism), by which we become **adopted children of God**, members of the Church and his adopted brothers and sisters. It is this life that is **supernatural**, since it surpasses the natural order and has, as its goal, **friendship with God** in the company of the saints. Even those natural goods, such as bliss and immortality sought by the pagans, only find their proper place in this life of grace.

Although the term 'supernatural' only became widespread in theology after the work of **St Thomas Aquinas** (d. 1274), what is denoted by this word has always been present in Christianity and has had a profound impact on Western culture. For example, Christian writings of all centuries have given great emphasis to the virtues of *caritas* ('divine love') and **humility**, virtues bound up with the supernatural life that were practically unknown to pagan philosophy. One of the most obvious impacts of *caritas* on culture has been the development of the concept of **charitable work**, founded on the conviction that every human being is one's brother or sister in the supernatural life of grace. Humility is shown by saints like **St Francis of Assisi** (d. 1226), who have great holiness while having nothing by worldly standards.

Three signs of the supernatural life are especially visible. First, much Western art (9C–17C) aims to express the supernatural life in a concrete way: the **halo**, for example, signifies grace and not mere natural goodness (see p. 47). Second, the **lives of the saints** (see p. 103) show the diverse glory of the supernatural life. Third, the supernatural life is often visibly **persecuted**. Hence many Christians have suffered for their faith, from ancient Rome to present day Iraq and Pakistan.

Catholicism and the supernatural life: the deeper connections

Catholic teaching about the supernatural life is drawn from Scripture but has also been articulated over centuries of tradition and given a formal expression by the teaching office of the Church. In referring to this supernatural life, St Peter says we become **'partakers of the divine nature'** (2 Pet 1:4). St Paul calls us **'co-heirs of Christ'** (Rom 8:17), **'temples of the Holy Spirit'** (1 Cor 3:16) and makes the following promise, *"What no eye has seen, nor ear heard, nor the human heart conceived, what God has prepared for those who love him"* (1 Cor 2:9). In other words, what God offers is 'supernatural', in the sense that it is beyond any natural conception or desire. Other key passages are those in which Jesus states that the conduct of his disciples must exceed the natural order of goodness, *"But I say to you, Love your enemies and pray for those who persecute you, so that you may be sons of your Father who is in heaven"* (Mt 5:44). Such passages all indicate the offer of what is 'above nature', a gift that the Church Fathers refer to as **divinisation**, and our elevation to this state as the principal aspect of our **justification** in Christ.

To the modern mind, the word 'supernatural' implies power, an association reinforced by the anti-Christian philosopher Nietzsche (d. 1900) and many fictional 'superheroes'. By contrast, the Catholic understanding is that the basis and goal of the supernatural life is friendship with God. As Aquinas says, *"If anyone has a Gift of the Holy Spirit without having the Spirit, the water is not united with its source, and so is not living but dead"* (Super Io., 4, 2). In other words, the gifts of the supernatural life are inseparable from the person of the giver. It is in the context of this friendship that *caritas* (divine love) and humility (which keeps us united to God) are central virtues.

An image of a child in the womb

Remarkable advances in medical research and imaging technology have underlined the way in which an unborn child is not simply an extension of his or her mother, but begins to act from conception as a living, growing being. All human beings reading these words today are beneficiaries of the fact that their own lives were not terminated prematurely by human choice. Yet the Catholic Church often stands almost alone in defending the sanctity of human life from conception to natural death, frequently seeking alternative means to support those contemplating abortion.

The Sanctity of Life

"Here there cannot be Greek and Jew, circumcised and uncircumcised, barbarian, Scythian, slave, free man, but Christ is all, and in all."

Col 3:11.

The Catholic record

The word 'sanctity' means the quality of being sacred or holy. The principle that a human person is **inherently sacred** has been one of the distinctive marks of Christian ethics since the beginning of the faith, a stance that has brought the Church into conflict, on many occasions, with non-Christian culture.

This conflict has been most apparent in the case of those persons unable to defend their own right to exist. One of the earliest Christian texts (late 1C/early 2C), the *Didache*, states, *"You shall not murder a child by abortion nor kill that which is begotten"* (II). So the first Christians **opposed abortion and infanticide**, which were widely practised in the Roman world, and Christians strove in later centuries against pagan cultures that practised child sacrifice. As noted previously, Scripture mentions that **widows** were given help and a role in the early Church (Acts 6:1-2; 9,39), an indication of a special respect for those often despised by society. The principle of sanctity also extended to one's own life. In contrast to general Greco-Roman culture, early Christians regarded **suicide as evil** (St Augustine, *City of God*, 1.20) and honoured the mortal remains of the dead with **burial**, often in catacombs close to saints.

Attitudes towards slaves are further evidence of a new, **universal** sense of the sanctity of life. The Roman Varro (d. 27 BC) described a slave as a 'speaking tool' (*instrumentum vocale*). St Paul in his Letter to Philemon, by contrast, writes to the master of a runaway slave with these words, "*Perhaps this is why he (Onesimus) was parted from you (Philemon) for a while, that you might have him back for ever, no longer as a slave but more than a slave, as a beloved brother, especially to me but how much more to you, both in the flesh and in the Lord.*" This spirit of common sonship sowed the seed of an idea that would eventually make slavery abhorrent in many parts of the world. An early example of this change is the way in which a Roman noblewoman, **St Perpetua**, and her slave, **St Felicity**, both died as sisters in the faith in 203 AD. **St Patrick** (d. c. 461), who had been a slave himself, preached against slavery. Following the collapse of the Roman Empire, slavery did decline in the Middle Ages as serfdom slowly rose, only to return again in more modern times. **St Peter Claver** (d. 1654) worked to assist slaves and **St Josephine Bakhita** (d. 1947) was herself a slave.

Over recent years, a decline of the Catholic faith has often been correlated with a decline of respect for the sanctity of life. Virulently anti-Christian states, such as Communist or National Socialist (Nazi) societies, have been responsible for some of the gravest attacks on the sanctity of life. Yet similar trends are evident in many countries today. The United Kingdom, for example, de-criminalised suicide in 1961 and abortion in 1967. Today in Britain, more than one in five pregnancies end in abortion, the destruction of human embryos and prenatal eugenic selection is commonplace and there is growing pressure to legalise euthanasia. In many countries, such opposition as exists to these trends comes invariably from Catholics or evangelical Christians.

Catholicism and the sanctity of life: the deeper connections

The principle of the sanctity of life in Scripture is linked with a person's relationship to God, a relationship that begins before birth, *"Before I formed you in the womb I knew you, and before you were born I consecrated you"* (Jer 1:5). Furthermore, in the Gospel of Luke, the first person to witness to the Incarnation is an unborn child, John, who leaps in his mother's womb at the presence of Mary, the mother of Jesus, *"When the voice of your greeting came to my ears, the babe in my womb leaped for joy"* (Lk 1:44). In other words, God's relationship to a person begins before birth and even **prenatal human life is sacred** to him.

This notion of being 'sacred', however, goes far beyond God thinking that human life is a good thing. Jesus describes the verdict given on the Day of Judgment as follows, *"Truly, I say to you, as you did it to one of the least of these my brethren, you did it to me"* (Mt 25:40). In other words, the Son of God goes so far as to identify good and evil done to other persons as good and evil also done to him. So good and evil done to persons is of the greatest significance for our own eternal destiny.

This relationship to God and our eternal destiny are the basis of many **Catholic teachings about persons**. For example, the alleviation of pain is good, but it is not right to deprive the dying person of consciousness without a serious reason (*Declaration on Euthanasia*, 1980) – let alone deliberately end that life – since the **last moments of life** can be a crucial opportunity to prepare for eternity. Only in the case of grave threats to society as a whole can a public authority order actions that may lead to the death of persons, such as declaring **war**, and even then there are moral constraints on acceptable actions.

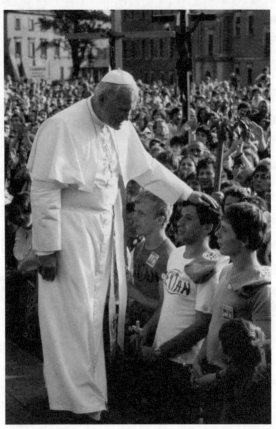

Pope John Paul II, visiting his native Poland in June 1979,
the first visit by a pontiff to a Communist-ruled country

The extraordinary response to the visit of the Holy Father to Poland helped
to promote popular but also largely peaceful opposition to Communist rule
in Eastern Europe, culminating with the fall of the Berlin Wall in 1989.

Deliverance from Evil

"We felt that we had received the sentence of death; but that was to make us rely not on ourselves but on God who raises the dead; he delivered us from so deadly a peril, and he will deliver us." 2 Cor 1:9-10.

The Catholic record

This section presents extraordinary deliverances, connected with the Catholic faith. By these events, persons and societies experiencing persecution have been rescued from what has felt like a sentence of death beyond human hope of remedy.

Some of these deliverances have involved armed resistance. Heavily outnumbered Catholic forces defeated invaders in several of the most critical battles of history, including **Tours** (732), the **Siege of Malta** (1565), **Lepanto** (1571) and **Vienna** (1683). Catholic Poland also defeated the Red Army unexpectedly in the **Battle of Warsaw** (1920), saving many countries from possible invasion and communist dictatorship.

Other kinds of deliverance are remarkable insofar as they have taken place without any military force at all. **Pope St Leo the Great** (d. 461), for example, persuaded Attila the Hun to turn back from his threatened attack on Rome (452) and later mitigated the sack of the city by the Vandals (455). In more recent times, **Bl. Bishop von Galen** (d. 1946) the 'Lion of Münster', denounced euthanasia and arbitrary arrests and killings by the Nazis. He was placed under house arrest but succeeded in halting the euthanasia programme in Westphalia for a time. **Pope Pius XII** (d. 1958) is often accused of not doing more to save Jews from the Nazis. Yet in 1945, Chief Rabbi Herzog wrote, *"The people of Israel will never forget what His Holiness and his illustrious delegates, inspired by the eternal principles of religion which form the very foundation of true civilization, are doing for our unfortunate brothers and sisters in the most tragic hour of our history."* **Bl. Pope John Paul II** (d. 2005) is widely credited for helping to bring about the **peaceful collapse of communism** in Europe. In 1979, the Holy Father celebrated Mass before three million of his countrymen, a previously unthinkable event behind the Iron Curtain. By giving impetus to peaceful change, he also helped to ensure that the end of communism did not trigger a global war, possibly with nuclear weapons

The Catholic Church herself has also been under the sentence of death on many occasions, but has confounded expectations by rising from the grave. From the 1530s onwards the Reformation nearly annihilated the ancient Catholic faith of England. Henry VIII destroyed the entire medieval monastic system and the subsequent Penal Laws of Elizabeth I and her successors, throughout the British Isles, were savagely brutal. Yet today the Catholic Church is the largest Christian body in the country, in terms of numbers regularly attending services. Similarly in France, many faithful Catholics suffered severe persecution or were put to death after the Revolution. Yet in the following century France produced hundreds of new religious congregations and great saints such as **Jean-Marie Vianney** (d. 1859), **Bernadette Soubirous** (d. 1879) and **Thérèse of Lisieux** (d. 1897). In the 20C the Church has faced persecutions in Armenia, under the Nazis and Communists, in Islamic countries such as Sudan and Pakistan, and even in Catholic countries like Spain and Mexico.

At the beginning of the 21C, the Catholic faith is still under threat worldwide. Converts to Catholicism face the death penalty in several countries, mainly in the Middle East. In the Far East, the Church can barely operate at all in North Korea and is in conflict with the Chinese communist government over the freedom to appoint bishops. Certain recent laws in Western countries have forced faithful Catholics out of their jobs or vocational work. In England, for example, a new Equality Law (2009) forced all Catholic adoption agencies to close down or sever ties with the Church, for refusing to place children with homosexual couples. Christian couples who have refused to condone homosexual behaviour have subsequently been barred by law from adopting. To give another example, the Swedish Parliament voted on 11 May 2011 to campaign against a European resolution upholding the right to conscientious objection to abortion. Yet the lesson of history is that the work of the Gospel will continue and that the faith will remain supernaturally fruitful.

Catholicism and deliverance from evil: the deeper connections

At the root of the Catholic understanding of deliverance from evil is **the death and Resurrection of Christ**. Just as Christ appeared to be defeated on Calvary and then broke the chains of death, the Church has often appeared to be defeated, only to rise again from the ashes. Indeed, one might almost claim that the vocation of the Christian is to be defeated, since Christian fruitfulness is rooted in the principle of 'survival of the faithful' not 'survival of the fittest'. Despite the many mistakes and failures of members of the Church to live up to this ideal, it is **divine love and sacrifice**, not materialist power, that ultimately defeats evil and produces lasting fruit.

Ss Cyril and Methodius (9C), who devised the first alphabet suited to the features of the Slavonic language. Their work was subsequently developed into the Cyrillic alphabet, the standard alphabet of many Slavic and non-Slavic languages today, including Russian, Bulgarian, Serbian, Ukrainian, Kazakh and Mongolian.

Language

The multitude came together and they were amazed and wondered, saying, "Are not all these who are speaking Galileans? And how is it that we hear, each of us in his own native language?" Acts 2:6-8.

The Catholic record

Catholic civilisation has made profound contributions to the development and use of language. The fact that Greek and Latin have a central place in the faith is significant because these languages are based on true **alphabets**. Languages written with alphabets facilitate popular literacy. Letters are easier to learn than the symbols of 'logographic' languages, such as Chinese, and their inclusion of vowels enables words to be formed and understood with little or no context. The **Latin alphabet**, which Catholic missionaries helped to disseminate to the Americas, Africa, Asia and Australia, is now the most widely used alphabetic writing system in the world. Furthermore, the Latin alphabet has been used to write down many indigenous languages for the first time.

Besides spreading Latin and Greek, Catholic civilisation also helped to develop three other major alphabetic systems. **St Mesrop Mashtots** (d. 440) helped to fix the form of the **Armenian language**, which was first used for a translation of the Bible. The accessibility of Scripture also motivated the development of the **Georgian alphabet** in the 4C/5C. Two missionaries of the 9C, **Ss Cyril and Methodius**, are credited with shaping the prototype of the **Cyrillic alphabet**, now the principal alphabet of Slavonic languages such as Russian. Since alphabets also need to be recognisable, it is not surprising that Catholic civilisation also developed standard **scripts**. These scripts include **Carolingian minuscule** (9C – 12C) with its well-rounded shapes, distinguishable forms, capital letters and spaces, and **Gothic ('Black Letter') minuscule** (from 12C), a more compact script to meet the needs of growing literacy and the university system.

Starting from the 6C, Catholic Europe also developed what were later called **grammar schools** to teach Latin, the language of scholarship in the Middle Ages and early modern times. In the 12C, these schools became the entry points to a liberal arts education at the new universities (see p. 40).

Catholic civilisation has also generated or influenced many vernacular languages, especially the Romance languages, a group that includes **Italian**, **Spanish**, **French** and **Portuguese**. Catholicism provided the cultural framework for the *Divina Commedia* ('Divine Comedy'), the *Cantar de Mio Cid* ('The Song of my Lord') and *La Chanson de Roland* ('The Song of Roland'), vernacular works that greatly influenced the development of Italian, Spanish and French respectively.

The complex history of **English** is interwoven with Catholicism. All early Anglo-Saxon texts are influenced by the faith, *Cædmon's Hymn* (7C) being arguably the earliest extant work of Old English. Catholicism has also contributed to a rich English **nomenclature**, for example: **Christmas** (from 'the Mass of Christ'); **Preston** (from 'Priests' town'); **Blackfriars** (from the 'Black Friars' of the Dominican Order); **Michaelmas** and **Hilary terms** (from the feasts of Ss Michael and Hilary); **Marigold** (from 'Mary's gold') and

Our Lady's Mantle (referring to the Virgin Mary). Many pub names like **Bishop's Mitre**, **Cross Keys** (a symbol of the Papacy) and **Lion and Lamb** are Catholic. Many first names also owe their popularity to the names of famous saints.

Catholics also developed the first techniques to enable the blind to read. **Valentin Haüy** (d. 1822), brother of the Abbé Haüy (the priest who invented crystallography), founded the **first school for the blind**. A student from this school, **Louis Braille** (d. 1852), simplified their system of raised writing to create the Braille system, which is now used worldwide.

Catholicism and language: the deeper connections

Catholicism is intimately associated with language, and Jesus Christ is even described as the 'Word' (Jn 1:1). The faith is communicated largely, though not exclusively, through words and the faith has inspired a great deal of writing throughout its long history, starting with the books of the New Testament. Furthermore, given the need to communicate universally, without restriction to any particular region or group, members of the Church have made great efforts to develop and translate languages. As an example of the sacrifices made to overcome such barriers, **St Jerome** (d. 420) spent twenty-three years writing an accurate Latin translation of Scripture (the **Vulgate**) from Greek and Hebrew. Missionary orders continue to make extraordinary efforts to overcome language barriers in many parts of the world today.

From this inspiration to communicate the faith, and for the Church worldwide to pray and work in harmony, it is not surprising that Catholicism has been so fruitful in the translation, development and even invention of languages.

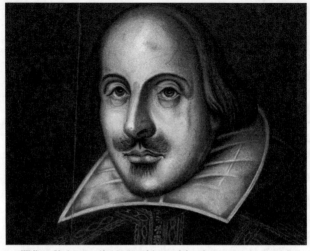

William Shakespeare (d. 1616), widely regarded as the pre-eminent writer of the English language and the world's greatest dramatist

Although Shakespeare left us little direct evidence of his religious views, he wove many Catholic themes into his plays, such as Hamlet's references to Purgatory. These literary clues, together with certain details of his life and family, have given increased credence to modern claims that he tried his best to live and die as a Catholic at a time of severe persecution, when offering Mass in England was punishable by death. Certainly the following lament over England would have resonated immediately with Catholics who were seeing their country go to war against her own ancient faith:

> *... Of the world's ransom, blessed Mary's Son,*
> *This land of such dear souls, this dear dear land,*
> *Dear for her reputation through the world,*
> *Is now leased out, I die pronouncing it,*
> *Like to a tenement or pelting farm:*
>
> *... That England, that was wont to conquer others,*
> *Hath made a shameful conquest of itself*
>
> *Richard II*, Act II, Scene 1

Literature and Poetry

"All scripture is inspired by God and profitable for teaching, for reproof, for correction, and for training in righteousness" (2 Tim 3:16); *"An inscription also was written over him in letters of Greek, Latin, and Hebrew."* Lk 23:38.

The Catholic record

Catholicism from the beginning has inspired a vast and imaginative literary culture. The writings of the New Testament were completed within seventy years of Christ's death and volumes of early Christian writings, letters, sermons, treatises, dialogues and hagiography followed over the next three centuries. St Augustine's *Confessions* can be called the first **autobiography**. This new genre moves beyond the mere facts and deeds of ancient chronicles and puts the relationship of a soul to God at the heart of the narrative. This new 'personalism' later inspired the invention of the **novel**, rooted in medieval romances which were inspired by the themes of love, the soul and eternity.

The Middle Ages produced an outpouring of literary genius, shaped by a Catholic outlook and the drama of salvation. The **first poem in the English language** is the *Hymn of Caedmon*, and the *Dream of the Rood* is a very early Anglo-Saxon poem about the cross of Christ. Later in the English Catholic tradition we find **William Langland, Chaucer** and the converts **Crashaw, Dryden** and **Alexander Pope**. Catholic themes also influenced the plays of **Shakespeare**.

A Catholic understanding of the way of salvation, the love of God and the battle against evil have also inspired what is arguably the **greatest poem of all time**, the *Divine Comedy* of Dante Alighieri (d. 1361). Dante's greatness is not simply found in his brilliant style and paradigmatic form of the Italian language but rather his penetrating themes. He takes his reader through the vast eternal states of Hell and Heaven and through the transitory journey up Mount Purgatory and understands human existence through divine love. Dante's insights into the drama of the soul have had a powerful and enduring impact on culture.

In more recent times, a devout Catholic, J. R. R. Tolkien (d. 1973), wrote **the most popular book of the twentieth century, *The Lord of the Rings*.** The centrality of the faith to Tolkien's life can be seen by these words, written to his son, shortly before his death, "*I put before you the one great thing to love on earth: the Blessed Sacrament ... There you will find romance, glory, honour, fidelity, and the true way of all your loves upon earth.*" Tolkien's great trilogy is a tale shot through with divine providence and many other themes of Christian thought, such as victory over evil coming through fidelity, love and sacrifice rather than physical strength.

Other influential Catholic writers of recent times include **Francis Marion Crawford, Robert Hugh Benson, Evelyn Waugh, Flannery O'Connor, Graham Greene, Gilbert Keith Chesterton, Hiliare Belloc, Maurice Baring** and **Piers Paul Reid.** Recent Catholic poets have included **Gerard Manley Hopkins, Francis Thompson** and **Edith Sitwell**. Catholic themes also feature in the work of **Siegfried Sassoon** and **Oscar Wilde**, both of whom also converted to the faith before they died.

Catholicism, literature and poetry: the deeper connections

The fact that the Bible is integral to the Catholic faith, and that **Scripture** is often written in narrative or poetic form, has provided a great inspiration for the creation of literature and poetry. In addition, poetry is a special fruit of prayer in at least three ways. First, poetry arises from a mind that is open to wonder, a state that is encouraged by faith, contemplation and prayer. Second, the approach to God through **prayer and ritual** is often couched in similar symbolism and metaphor as is found in poetry. Third, the Catholic prayer book, the Divine Office or Breviary, is based upon the poetic tradition of the Old Testament. The fruits of centuries of immersion in these prayers are evident in the poetry of the Middle Ages.

Furthermore, the themes of a Catholic understanding of the world, and the metaphors by which those themes are expressed, have been an evident inspiration to many of the authors cited above. The stories of Graham Greene, for example, are clearly inspired by God, life and death, mortal sin and the state of grace, hell and heaven. By contrast, on the subject of modernist authors who neglected such themes, Greene wrote that the characters they devised "*wandered about like cardboard symbols through a world that is paper-thin.*"

This 'flatness' of characters and stories, at least as Greene describes it, is plausibly due to the loss of Christian themes. If, after all, our existence is accidental, with no greater purpose, then poetry and literature are little more than the grunts of clever apes doomed to die and be lost forever. With the spread of such views today, it is not surprising that much literature of the modern age reflects a kind of despair.

*An example of Gregorian Chant from a medieval manuscript,
showing the recording of music using early staff notation*

From at least the 12C, early monastic plainchant notation developed into staff notation, the system of horizontal lines, notes and annotations which today provides the universal language for reading and writing music. As with many fruits of Catholic civilisation, the musical notation system is largely taken for granted yet has incalculable importance. Without such a system, none of the complex works of the great composers would have been possible or performable, and music could not have been preserved through history.

Music

"Be filled with the Spirit, addressing one another in psalms and hymns and spiritual songs, singing and making melody to the Lord with all your heart, always and for everything giving thanks …" Eph 5:18-20.

The Catholic record

St Augustine (d. 430) claimed, *"To sing is the work of a lover,"* and *"The one who sings prays twice,"* and it is no exaggeration to say that Catholic worship was the foundation of the western musical tradition. Drawing initially from the Psalms, canticles of Scripture and Jewish antecedents, liturgical music from the sixth century developed into monophonic music called **Gregorian chant**, named after **Pope Gregory the Great** (d. 604). This chant is still used in liturgy today and has recently gained broader popularity. Monks also developed methods for recording chant on parchment, techniques which led to the invention of **staff notation** and the 'ut-re-mi' (**do-re-mi**) mnemonic by the Benedictine monk **Guido of Arezzo** (d. 1003). These inventions were of incalculable significance for the preservation, teaching and development of music.

Cathedral schools from the tenth century developed early **polyphony**, a form of music that harmonised and alternated voices in chant. Key documents from this period include the *Winchester Troper* (c. 1000), the oldest extant example of notated polyphony, and the *Magnus Liber Organi*, attributed to the masters of the Notre Dame school of music such as

Léonin and **Pérotin** (12C/13C). After a brief period of some doubt about the suitability of polyphony for the Mass, **De Machaut** (d. 1377), composed the *Messe de Notre Dame* for Rheims cathedral, creating the first polyphonic Mass that is also the first known instance of a unified musical composition by one person. Two exemplars of mature sacred polyphony are **Palestrina** (d. 1594) and **Victoria** (d. 1611).

Tallis (d. 1585) and **Byrd** (d. 1623) took polyphonic music to new heights of sophistication, despite some hostility to such music in post-Reformation England. Working under the protection of Royal patronage, Byrd composed Masses for three, four, and five voices to be used by Catholics at secret Masses. At the pinnacle of polyphonic virtuosity, Tallis wrote *Spem in Alium* for forty voices and **Striggio's** (d. 1592) *Missa Sopra Ecco* even uses sixty voices for the final *Agnus Dei*.

Another musical genre rooted in Catholic culture is the lyric poem called a **hymn**. Early Latin hymns include *Stabat Mater* of **Jacopone da Todi** (d. 1306) and *Adoro Te Devote* of **St Thomas Aquinas** (d. 1274). Although they are often associated with the Reformation, Germany also had over 1400 **vernacular hymns** before Luther's time. Catholic hymn writers of more modern times include **Caswall** (d. 1878), **Newman** (d. 1890), **Faber** (d. 1863) and **Hopkins** (d. 1899).

Another genre with Catholic origins is the **oratorio**, the beginnings of which are associated with the Oratory of St Philip Neri (d. 1593). Famous oratorios include Handel's *Messiah* and *The Dream of Gerontius*, a poem by Bl. Cardinal Newman set to music by the Catholic composer **Elgar** (d. 1934). Another Catholic composer, **Haydn** (d. 1809) strongly influenced the development of the **symphony** and **string quartet**. Yet another famous genre from Catholic civilisation is the **opera**, which started in Italy with the work of **Jacopo Peri** (d. 1633), and soon spread throughout Europe.

Many of the fruits of Catholic culture extend well beyond confessional borders. **J. S. Bach** (d. 1750) wrote music for Lutheran liturgies that borrowed many elements from the Mass, and one of his last works was his *Mass in B minor*. The forms of the liturgy, and Church patronage, also shaped and enabled many works by **Monteverdi** (d. 1643), **Vivaldi** (d. 1741), **Mozart** (d. 1791) and **Beethoven** (d. 1827). The great *Symphony No. 8* of **Mahler** (d. 1911) takes as its principal theme the ancient hymn of Pentecost, *Veni creator spiritus*.

Catholicism and music: the deeper connections

The intimate connection of music with liturgy and prayer is clear from the psalms and many references in Scripture, for example, *"And when they (Jesus and the apostles) had sung a hymn, they went out to the Mount of Olives"* (Mt 26:30). Scripture also associates music with the vision of heaven, *"And I heard a voice from heaven like the sound of many waters and like the sound of loud thunder; the voice I heard was like the sound of harpers playing on their harps, and they sing a new song before the throne"* (Rev 14:2-3).

Exactly why music is so linked in its origins to prayer is not easy to determine, mainly because the nature and power of music remain surprisingly mysterious. Music seems to be something we *join*, which shapes our sympathies to align with those with whom we share the experience (Scruton, *Understanding Music*, p. 54). This description is similar to the saints' descriptions of being moved by the Holy Spirit, suggesting that holy music is naturally consonant with a deep sense of union with God.

Pope John Paul II in the year 2000, when he acknowledged many evils committed by members of the Church through the centuries

The Church brings the freedom of forgiveness to sinners, but the members of the Church have frequently to acknowledge and ask forgiveness for their own sins. Forgiveness and receiving forgiveness are among the most distinctive marks of Catholic societies, and the difficulties, sacrifices and drama of forgiveness have profoundly influenced literature and art.

Forgiveness

"Forgive us our trespasses as we forgive those who trespass against us" (Mt 6:12); *"My son, your sins are forgiven"* (Mk 2:5); *"Father, forgive them; for they know not what they do."* Lk 23:34.

The Catholic record

Forgiveness, both received and granted, is one of the key fruits of the Catholic faith. No less than **four sacraments**, out of seven, are devoted, wholly or in part, to forgiveness. The faith also teaches that all Christians, by virtue of Baptism, have received **complete forgiveness** of all sin at least once in their lives, and the history of Christianity is replete with dramatic examples of forgiveness. By means of forgiveness, even some of the greatest sinners have become great saints.

The unnamed thief who asked Christ for mercy, even while crucified beside him, received Christ's promise, *"Today you will be with me in paradise"* (Lk 23:43), giving the hope of forgiveness, even at the very end of life, to all generations. **St Peter the Apostle** received the forgiveness of Christ after denying him three times, going on to lead the Church and finally to lay down his life for the Lord. **Saul of Tarsus** (**St Paul**, d. c. 67), who had previously organised the persecution of Christians, went on to become the great missionary to the Gentiles and also died for the faith. **St Augustine of Hippo** (d. 430), who had previously led an immoral life, received baptism from St Ambrose and went on to become a bishop and one of the greatest Doctors of the Church. **Constantine the Great** (d. 337) was baptised, albeit just before he died, becoming the first Christian Emperor. The **Emperor Theodosius** (d. 395), having massacred thousands of citizens, did severe public penance at the behest of St Ambrose and finally received forgiveness, teaching the world that political power cannot be exercised free of moral constraint. **St Margaret of Cortona** (d. 1297), was converted from an immoral life and suffered frequent temptations, yet she joined the Third Order of St Francis, confronted an immoral bishop, and today her body lies incorrupt. Another convert from a wasteful life was **St Ignatius of Loyola** (d. 1556), founder of the Jesuits. The poet **Francis Thompson** (d. 1907) left a life of opium addiction and vice and spoke of God pursuing him 'like the hound of heaven' unto forgiveness. The journalist **Malcolm Muggeridge** (d. 1990) converted after an early life that had been morally and intellectually hostile to Christ. Similarly, **Oscar Wilde** (d. 1900) was received into the Church before he died, having previously written, in Reading Gaol, "*How else but through a broken heart may Lord Christ enter in?*" **John Wayne** (d. 1979) also converted to the faith before his death. A former London gangster, **John Pridmore,** recently converted and now devotes his life to preaching the gospel.

In preparation for the third Christian millennium, **Pope John Paul II** also invited members of the Church to "*purify themselves, through repentance, of past errors and instances of infidelity, inconsistency and slowness to act.*" In one of many acts to heal past wounds, he became the first Pope to visit the synagogue of Rome, describing the Jews as 'elder brothers'. More recently, **Pope Benedict XVI** has called for the same repentance and reparation with regard to the 'unspeakable crimes' of abuse.

Besides these private and public acts of reconciliation, this emphasis on forgiveness has permeated cultures shaped by the faith. For example, the word 'forgive' comes from an old English word *forgiefan*, a word which means to 'give completely' or 'to give in marriage'. The choice of this word and its implications reflects a Catholic sense of the restoration of **communion with God**. The theme of forgiveness has also been fruitful in literature. **Shakespeare** (d. 1616), for example, who is believed by many to have been Catholic, wrote the following lines in praise of mercy, *"The quality of mercy is not strain'd. It droppeth as the gentle rain from heaven upon the place beneath: it is twice blest; it blesseth him that gives and him that takes … it is an attribute of God himself"* (The Merchant of Venice, IV.1).

Catholicism and forgiveness: the deeper connections

The ultimate root of Christian forgiveness is the **love and sacrifice of Christ on Calvary**, when the sinless Son of God offered up his life to save sinners. The forgiveness that flourishes from this root is shown by numerous passages of the New Testament in which Jesus forgives sins, teaches forgiveness, tells parables about forgiveness and grants his apostles the gift of forgiving sins. Forgiveness is also the subject of the only conditional petition of the *Our Father* and Jesus' solemn warning, *"If you forgive others their trespasses, your heavenly Father will also forgive you; but if you do not forgive others, neither will your Father forgive your trespasses"* (Matt 6:14-15). In other words, a failure to forgive could cause a person to lose eternal life. Given the many centuries that the Church has taught Christ's words and made the sacraments available for the forgiveness of sins, it is not surprising that forgiveness has transformed many lives and permeated Christian culture.

The saints in heaven, detail from The Last Judgment by Fra Angelico, painted c. 1430 and now in the museum of San Marco in Florence

While the saints are perfect in their love of God, their distinctions as persons remain in heaven and each one has a unique glory. The Catholic understanding that the saints genuinely co-operate with God's grace is opposed to any sense of fatalism about salvation or the world. This understanding also encourages Christians to continue to grow and be spiritually fruitful to the last moment of earthly life.

The Saints

"They shall be his people, and God himself will be with them; he will wipe away every tear from their eyes, and death shall be no more ... for the former things have passed away." Rev 21:3-4.

The Catholic record

The 'saints' are those human persons who are now in heaven, where they see God face to face. While the number and names of all the saints are unknown, the Church formally recognises that certain persons are definitely in heaven. These persons receive the appellation '**Saint**' and can be asked to intercede or pray for those still on earth.

Since the Church is established on earth to gather humanity to divine life in heaven, a saint is **the most important fruit of the faith**. Indeed, Bl. John Henry Newman (d. 1890) described the work of the Church in these words, *"That mighty world-wide Church, like her Divine Author, regards, consults for, labours for the individual soul ... Her one duty is to bring forward the elect to salvation"* (Lectures on Anglican Difficulties, VIII.3). In other words, every facet of the Catholic faith, including its sacraments, teachings, hierarchy, laws and so on, exists to create saints. While the saints are the principal fruits and glory of the kingdom of heaven, many saints have also exercised a profound influence in civil matters, as, for example, scholars, teachers, carers, monarchs and sources of inspiration. A plethora of place names worldwide testify to the cultural impact of saints.

The diversity of the saints is one of their most striking characteristics. Saints include men and women, children and the aged, single and married persons, kings and beggars, ordained, religious and members of the laity. There have been many ways of classifying saints, but the liturgy of the Church recognises the following major categories. First, there is the **Virgin Mary**, who is given a unique place of honour as the Mother of Jesus. Then there are the **apostles**, principally the twelve apostles called by Christ: Peter, Andrew, James, John, John, Philip, Bartholomew (Nathanael), Matthew (Levi), Thomas, James (son of Alphaeus), Thaddeus (Jude) and Simon the Zealot with Matthias replacing Judas, who betrayed Jesus. St Paul, the 'Apostle to the Gentiles' is also classified in the liturgy as an apostle, while some pioneering missionaries are given the honorific title 'apostles': Saint Augustine of Canterbury is sometimes called the 'Apostle to the English'.

A second major group of saints are the **martyrs**, who were put to death for bearing witness to Christ and his teaching. The many martyrs include the Holy Innocents, the deacon Stephen, the widow Anastasia, the statesman Thomas More, the wife and mother Margaret Clitherow and the priest Andrew Kim Taegon. The twentieth century produced more martyrs than all other centuries combined, two prominent examples being Maximilian Kolbe and Edith Stein, both of whom died in the Nazi concentration camp of Auschwitz.

A third group of saints are **virgins**, such as Agatha, Lucy, Agnes, Cecilia and Bernadette, who are honoured not simply for abstinence but for complete spousal devotion to God. These saints bear powerful witness, especially in a world of sexual vice, to a joyful, supernatural love of God. Such saints are also a special inspiration to female religious orders.

A fourth category includes many saints who were **pastors**, such as John Vianney and Philip Neri. The **Doctors of the Church** comprise pastors and other saints, such as Teresa of Ávila, whose teachings are regarded as universally important.

Finally, there are those saints who do not fit into any of the other categories, with special recognition given to **saints noted for works of mercy** and to **educators**. In recent years, there has been increased interest in the cause of **married couples**, such as Louis and Zélie Martin. There are also many saints of everyday life who are not yet known to us.

Catholicism and saints: the deeper connections

While almost all Christians view eternal life with God as the goal of faith, Catholic theology gives specific reasons for the prominence of the saints. First, Catholicism teaches that salvation is not merely added externally by God (the classic Protestant view) but consists in becoming **holy within** through grace. In other words, a saint is someone who has not just been considered by God as holy, but has actually become holy and is worthy of honour. Second, Catholicism teaches that we are **free to co-operate with grace**, so that works done in a state of grace can be meritorious. We can therefore honour the saints for their victories, achieved by grace. Third, the Catholic concept of salvation emphasises **divine adoption**, whereby a Christian is an adopted child of God and therefore worthy of special honour. Fourth, the faith teaches that the Church herself is a living **communion**, uniting the faithful on earth, in purgatory and in heaven. Just as we can ask others on earth to pray for us, it is even more effective to ask the saints in heaven to intercede for us.

Subject index

110